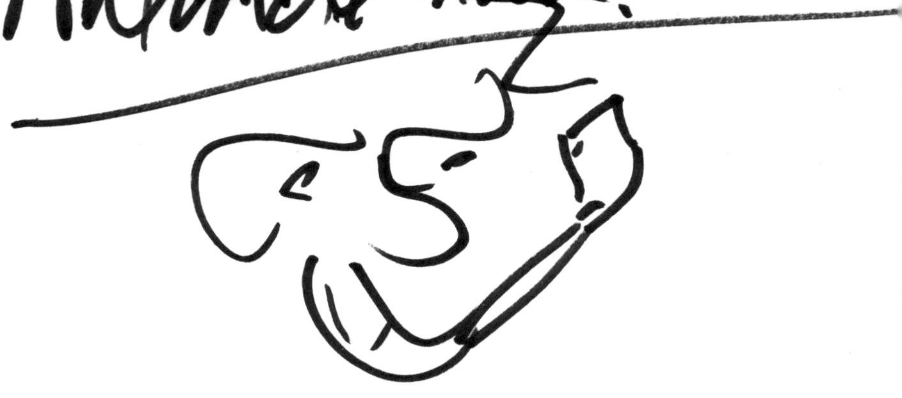

Eureka Productions
PO Box 4001
Truckee, CA 96160

92 Lafayette 3rd Floor
Brooklyn, NY 11217
www.eurekaproductions.tv

de Thouars, Willem
A Journey Through Time / Willem de Thouars
Manufactured in the United States of America.
ISBN-13: 978-0615710747 (Eureka Productions)
ISBN-10: 0615710743

A JOURNEY THROUGH TIME

WILLEM DE THOUARS

Sometimes it is good to be endorsed by someone – a friend, a good student or a famous individual – whose name carries a lot of weight. With my second book, I decided to ask my elders; to get their endorsements and ask how they relate to me as an individual over the years I had known them not just as students, but as friends and extended family. The write up I received from Professor David Conrad was certainly a plus for me. In my world it was never about me alone. I appreciate his contribution and his commentary. Professor Conrad, although well seasoned in other systems (such as fut ga kung fu and another stick fighting art of the Philippines), is always greatly admired as a student in my system. He is a practicing lawyer and a professor at the University of Denver.

–WILLEM DE THOUARS

* * *

A colleague at work recently asked me what style of Tai Chi Uncle practiced. I thought for a few moments and replied, "All of them." What I mean is that Uncle doesn't practice a particular style. He doesn't practice the Chen Style or the Hao Style or the Wu Style or the Long First Style or whatever. Instead, he has transcended the various styles to master the very heart, the very essence of Tai Chi. As a result, he practices Tai Chi without the attachment of any specific style.

Impressive enough to accomplish this with one art, Uncle has mastered multiple Chinese, Indonesian and European fighting arts. With each of these arts, he has gone beyond the art's particular style and mastered the art's true essence. I have seen him apply the same technique as a Tai Chi player, as a Bagua player, as a Serak player, as a Mantis player, as a Chamundi player, as a Kun Tao player, as a knife fighter, as a stick fighter, as a fencer, as a turn of the century boxer. The move is the same; just expressed differently according to each style. It is awe inspiring to watch.

Uncle is an equally gifted teacher as he is a martial artist. He is a modern day Socrates who doesn't train his students so much as helps his students discover their own art. He will show a technique; it is up to his students to figure out how he did it. The result is something that the student continually struggles with the ideas that Uncle is presenting. But once a student gets something, once the student has that flash of light, then the idea is part of the student's art forever.

In my life, I have never encountered anyone who is as good at anything as Uncle is practicing and teaching martial arts. I have been truly blessed to have him as my teacher.

–David Conrad, J.D., LLM in Taxation

* * *

Any endorsement of great individuals, like my students, is like blessings in the sky. Their opinions and the endorsement of this book are important to me and also for those reading this book. I have always tried to stay close to the truth as a teacher, to be sincere and to not hold back when I speak out, regardless of the consequences. This book is about history. The history of my teachers and the arts they taught me, but mostly about how history and its events are all part of the background of all martial arts.

Renee is the only capable and highly respected female practitioner and instructor to "spice up" my martial arts practices, both as a student and instructor. She is also my only female instructor. I appreciate her for who she is. I sincerely thank her for her endorsement of my book.

"I have had the privilege of training under Bapak Willem de Thouars for the past 9 years. During this time, I've come to learn that Uncle, as we affectionately call him, not only is a master of the fighting arts but is also an aficionado of history and provider of insights into everyday life. His two books reflect this. They describe the history of his teachers, illustrate his intense and longtime training, provide a general history lesson, and cast us pearls of wisdom along the way. By tying all these things together, he helps us to see the bigger picture of our martial arts training. His books are a necessary read for longtime practitioners of the martial arts and laypeople alike."

INTRODUCTION TO A LIFE'S JOURNEY

The Netherlands, a nation in Western Europe, had occupied the East Indian Archipelago for 360 years. The largest archipelago in the world consists of 16,000 islands and is part of the Malay Peninsula. The Malay Peninsula stretches from the shores of Japan to lands connected to Southeast Asia and to islands off the Australian continent.

To describe the Dutch East Indies appropriately you need to visualize the land. It thrives with luscious green forests, rich and productive soils, deep and fast streaming rivers. The rivers and forests teem with wildlife. The largest islands of the group are Sumatra, Borneo, Celebes, Java and Western New Guinea. Besides mountains, the tropical environment in this part of the southwest Pacific has many active volcanoes.

In 1948, independence from the Dutch came. Holland, under pressure from the United Nations and the United States, returned power to the Indonesians. The Indonesian government, under Sukarno, took supreme jurisdiction over all the islands. The former colony was inhabited by various nomadic tribes that came thousands of years ago from many other lands and settled in the archipelago. Indonesia was always a melting pot comprised of different cultures, customs, traditions and languages.

Always shrouded in the mystery of their cultural backgrounds, they had to oppose colonial rule from the Dutch, Portuguese, English and Spaniards. During the 16th and 17th centuries, the Europeans came and invaded the islands due to the greater demand for spices. Coffee, in particular, was considered a delicacy and British merchants began selling coffee beans first in Tangiers, then throughout the world. The island of Java was the main source of coffee beans at one time.

The islands of Indonesia had the most natural resources in Southeast Asia and were best known for the island spices among European merchants. King Phillip of Spain enforced higher taxes and tariffs on all Dutch goods. Sea wars between the Portuguese, Spaniards, English and Dutch were unavoidable.

I often wondered how a small nation in Europe, a land made up of mud and polder and just three-quarters the size of Colorado and a population of 11 million, could conquer a country three times the size of Texas and a population of 60 million for 360 years. In the 13th century, Indonesia defeated the invading Mongolian Army in East Java. Kublai Khan came with 30,000 troops and was driven back. A major reason why the Dutch were always so successful was their stubbornness. The Dutch have the qualities of strong motivation, a willingness to understand, the urge to seek new endeavors and to build and improve ideas for enterprise.

Holland, during her peak of colonization, was strongly motivated to expand economically. It formed the East Indian Company and the Royal Dutch Colonial Army, comprised mostly of Dutch volunteers, native soldiers and Dutch Indonesians or Indo Eurasians. The main objective of the colonial Army was to protect and defend the Dutch interests in the Archipelago. With trading posts in Asia, Boston and the West Indies, Holland's increasing wealth in the spice trade was a stronghold. Through strife and struggle, the Netherlands held a strong dominance over the native Indonesians for nearly four centuries.

An interesting fact from their past was the Dutch enterprising culture, architectonics, works of art, agriculture and trading posts. As a nation, the Dutch found their heredity from the Frisians and Batavians. The history of Holland began to evolve in the first century when the first settlers came from Denmark and Germany and started to work the land. They have lived in the Northeast ever since where the sea deposited fertile clay. As occupants of a lower land mass far below sea level, they became ingenious at fighting the destructive waters and were able to make the land between the Rhine and Maas Rivers very productive for agriculture. As the old saying goes, "The Dutch made the sea their ally to nurture their land!"

People of the lowland, as the neighboring countries called them, considered the Dutch very enterprising. By the year 100, man took action by building earthworks, such as dikes and dunes, to keep out water. Thereafter, they became some of the best ship builders, navigators and traveling merchants. This is a major reason why their corporations always had plenty of trading posts around the world.

When the Dutch settlers first came to the Archipelago they had high hopes. In 1604, the islands were part of the Malay Peninsula. People who went to the East Indies were ambitious and had trades such as farming, carpentry, administration, metal work and land development. They built cities, communities, churches, schools, factories and plantations. In 1605, a new race of people was created by the Dutch through marriage or forced intimate relations between European men and native women. The offspring were referred to as Indo Eurasians or Dutch Indonesians. They made their own culture, customs and traditions.

Despite being loyal to Holland's interests, they had to survive under the most difficult circumstances of Dutch racial segregation and economic disasters. In 1948, when the Netherlands returned the land to the native people, there was a high cost. Fleeing refugees of men, women and children found themselves without a country in a land of uncertainty. Their experiences as individuals were tragic events by moving from one country to another. In particular, the elderly were affected. It was like transplanting and old tree into new soil!

This was a time of remarkable development in rebuilding the war torn countries in Europe, China and Japan as well as the evolving time of the 1950's and how the course of history changed the world forever. The involvement of the United Nations in Korea was to halt further communistic action. General Douglas MacArthur led his United Nations land forces with a surprise and successful landing on Pusan to capture Seoul, South Korea. Considered a police action to drive communism from the southern peninsula, the UN forces fought the North Korean forces to the 38th parallel. When General MacArthur sought further action to drive the North Koreans beyond the 38th parallel, China intervened and Chinese forces moved into action. They nearly succeeded in driving the UN forces back to the sea. General MacArthur was immediately fired by President Harry S. Truman out of his concern for public opinion and the possibility of the third World War.

After the Second World War, many unfortunate evens of human tragedy took place. Several Dutch Indonesians were unable to enter Holland and were forced to take refuge in temporary camps provided by the Italian government in Italy. The Netherlands, as a nation, was unprepared for receiving her unwanted Southeast Asian citizens and sent them back to Italy. Holland was still hampered with social and domestic problems. The little country was faced with a housing and food shortage for its own Dutch citizens. They were ill equipped to deal with an influx of immigrants. Barely able to feed its own population, the country had to recover and rebuild its towns and factories to stabilize their steep recession. Through the ingenious plan of American General George S. Marshall, many European countries, including the Netherlands, were able to bring back their welfare systems through economic assistance.

Crucial to the Dutch were the social reforms and economic recovery. With the great housing shortage, many hotels, motels and inns were converted to housing projects to receive 10,000 of Holland's unwanted Southeast Asian citizens. The younger generation of the Dutch Indonesian men found themselves drafted into the armed forces or sent to trade schools so they could earn an income. Later, they were all required to repay the Dutch welfare system. The trade schools were a good thing. They gave the men a chance to prepare themselves for job placements in Europe from Holland to Germany. Thousands of the unwanted citizens found steady employment in coal mining, machine shops and in the building trades. Cultural differences between the Dutch and her citizens of the Southwest Pacific created a difficult time period in Holland.

* * *

My greatest source of inspiration always came through the presence of my immediate family and many friends. Blood family is not of one's own choosing, but good and trusted friends become extended family of my own choosing. I prefer sharing my feelings with my good friends. Many of my friends have trained with me, in the arts I practice, and became my closest associates. Their names are too numerous to mention. I will always treasure them like gold! In my deep consideration of each of them and to the men and women practicing my arts for self defense, they are wonderful as individuals. I have never known any of them to lack the enthusiasm for hard work in training.

I see and observe beauty and grace, even in the students trained by my associates, when they are practicing the fighting arts. I have taught many in the US and elsewhere. To my many friends, wherever you are, you have my gratitude for your loyalty and friendship.

One individual I would like to forward my most sincere appreciation to is Don Ethan Miller. I would like to devote an entire paragraph to him. He totally inspired me with my writing in English. In no way can I be like him – a specific styled and philosophical writer that has gone beyond many other writers. His influence in creating my own way of expressing myself, in describing my feelings in words, are all contributing efforts to touch my free spirit. That writing is, after all, a thought expressed in feelings. Writing is very much like painting, dancing and music all fit together in harmony. Don is just like a walking dictionary when it comes to Shakespeare, the father of modern English, in drama, speech and literary context. I listen with open ears, whenever Don and I are engaged in our table conversations. My enjoyment has always been how Don speaks with the charm of a delightful man, particularly when he speaks in outrage and in a calm manner about something that makes him mad. What makes Don my close associate as a brother in arms is that, no matter what, I consider him as one of my best internal arts practitioners and a fellow teacher.

The most important person in my life will always be my wife. We have been together as man and wife, friend and soul mate and most intimately as one soul for 46 years. Joyce Helen de Thouars Deerns has always been in my deep consideration, the backbone of my life. It was never easy to live with me. I am just too much of a free spirited soul, like a stallion that dwells and gallops on the prairie. Quite often, in the world we live in, some have condemned me because they didn't understand me. The free expression of my heart is my behavior. I enjoy the free spirited life that no one can take away. Unfortunately, we live in a hypocritical world of condemnation and are restricted under rules and regulations!

In the very essence of life, there are no restrictions, except those in a court of law. By the book and for the book dictate one's life. In this, my second book, *A Life's Journey*, is about life and the escapades and adventures I had to experience. How time has changed my whole way of thinking to live an acceptable means while fitting into a society of rules.

In a true heart, the freedom of speech is also a limited acceptance for the truth. Are we really free in what is acceptable of a meaning or what is not an acceptance to accommodate the glare of a free spirit? Man shall never be free in an environment of our society when rules are enforced by those who made them.

Those boundaries of limitation to the freedom of man have been adopted by most governments since the fall of Rome. Rome fell due to the corruption of the Senate. As the world has grown up since then, it is still experiencing the same devaluation of truth. As a civilization, our freedom of speech is living a life of the free has restricted consequences. We may think we are free, but we are not!

Rules are rules and even in writing, there are many rules: standard language rules, spelling rules, style rules. In my way of thinking, I like to break all the rules. It is a void and as long as a reader understands my vocabulary of speaking, in the way I conduct my spoken words, it is also the way I clarify my written context. For the educated scholars, I am a lost cause. For the ones who understand me – they already know me!

I am not educated in measuring up to the value of scholars and highly schooled individuals. All I know is how to survive life by gaining wisdom. It is to stay simple, to stay practical and use lots of common sense! Some of the educators in colleges and universities act like educated circus clowns with a greater lack in social skills.

My gratitude for my daughter and family and also my son and his family. All my grandkids give me the most joy, when they spend time with me and empty my refrigerator with their healthy appetites.

–WILLEM DE THOUARS

A FOREWARD

At times glory can only be found in the soul of a man. Happiness on Earth is a self-expressed thought of imagination in someone's belief. I have lived in the U.S. since May, 1960.

As individuals, we are mostly faced with a pressured life, due to the circumstances we create by accident. There are also times that it was a major reason for living in a very complex and vast world endeavor. The pressure, as a contributing factor, is a main reason most individuals are getting a prediction of financial recession. Financial recessions are predominantly a heritage to venture in the human race.

Money is the root of all evil, so they say. And contrary to this statement is also life's comfort – not a luxury but a necessity. There is no tranquility without the comfort of a home.

Considering myself a lucky man of many adventures, I also consider my home life of family and friends. Most of my friends are my students. The majority are caring people and I care immensely about them.

New acquaintances are always on the horizon. You can become acquainted with people in numbers that exceed beyond one's imagination. Really good friends are exactly like a few drops of water in an empty bucket. When you are rich, you have many friends that turn up out of nowhere and "sweet talk" you until you become weightless. As soon as you are totally broke and are in the poor house, then there are no more friends. My closest friend always remains my friend and experienced that fact of life. When he was on the top and well to do, many came to drain him.

When I look at the street animals, from dogs to cats and other living species, my heart bleeds. They were abandoned by owners who were uncaring and heartless. One of the reasons I became an artist was to make these animals my movie stars. These animals and wild animals are in the stories I tell on paper or on canvas.

Sadly, in a man's life, sometimes one has to make a choice in their blood family or extended family. My extended family is my students. They are always the ones to brighten my life. The ones that have gone their own way for reasons of their own should never be seen as a heartbreak because we are all free spirited individuals with desires. We are free to like or dislike someone. I, too, had to terminate friendships with individuals I had known for many years. We could not stand and see eye-to-eye.

My foreword is meant to express my feelings and my appreciation for all my students and really close friends. Some information on world events I obtained through history books and through the internet.

–The author

PART 1
REVOLVING TIMES

Looking back at my life for what it was worth, you would top the range of my horizon in the wealth of experiences and I thank the Universe or God. As we may consider the Almighty as the Great Divine, He has made life for me the very best throughout the essence of my living existence. Life, as a spiritual force, is not comprehensive in regard to emotions or physical feelings. It only understands the nature as a force that strengthens the bond between life and death and one's belief in a natural way. One can only imagine reaching out to a spiritual life after death! Philosophically I also think differently than others in their beliefs. Men are supposed to be equal as living species and as part of the universal force that makes human beings human. Unfortunately, it would not be hard for me even to enhance the thinking that all men are equal to that. Individuals come to Mother Earth in different sizes and with different physical capabilities making every individual a totally different living being. In measuring up to standards in an educated world or the uneducated environment, everyone has different abilities and capabilities to make a better life for oneself. There are followers and there are leaders!

Life is anything else that concerns life and living it, my psychological reasoning behind my thoughts were the fortitude of suffering the real quality of a serene unity I tried to reach. A peaceful quality in which the body, mind and soul were harmoniously inclined to spirit and nature. Spiritually, it is true nature of form of a hidden "UNSEEN" that cannot be touched or felt. It is the true nature of our spiritual existence that attached itself to our sixth sense. Physically, each human being has a different body structure that can be seen or felt. Therefore, it is the total opposite way of thinking; an opposite in motivation and also an opposite in humanistic behaviorism from other individuals. Each of us as humans are here on Earth with a purpose and each of us inhabit a place in which we reside only to know that we are all here on borrowed time.

Perhaps of all the sports I had endeavored and all of the various qualities of a diverse sense in playing, the practice of really understanding the nature of a sporting activity through experiencing it was a time in my life. Each event made me more aware of my surroundings, and every sport is the total opposite of another sport.

This is the second book of my autobiography. It continuously moves forward with inspired thoughts for addressing issues that I have always kept to myself. Quite frankly, I actually have no issues in life. I only need to experience the "School of Reality" in what is real and in what is accepted as truth. This new book is all about the chapters, or episodes, in journeys through time and the aftermath of World War II.

My voyages have been quite rewarding experiences. To think that I started to travel around the world at age 17 by working on ships as a deck hand, then officer's steward, cook baker and lathe operator. Then there are the revolving moments, involving my adventuresome escapades from adolescence through maturity. I saw many continents and lands by peaking through the windows of airplanes. Consequently, by way of air travel, I was able to fly in any of the planes made by Boeing, Douglas or the Air Bush Industries in Europe.

Never overlook the fact that my Mongolian fighting arts teachers taught me useful practices: how to overcome hunger and to search my soul to survive. I undertook the field of fighting arts with a long road ahead. Each road had a steep climb in order for me to reach a top level, not without pain or strife in hard laboring efforts.

By endeavoring in the practice of training of fighting arts, it could be a difficult task to describe the training methodology of any art. After 67 years of putting a learned behavior into practice, it is quite often a difficult path to follow. Practicing the ways of the Old School Temple boxing styles was sometimes a sophisticated issue in how to seek answers from a teacher who disregarded the feelings of others and took acceptance only in the trauma of physical pain in hardship. It is an answer only shared when pain generates a comprehension of understanding.

After experiencing the traumas, the painstaking events in a loss of blood, could the magical word of comprehension be fully understood in appreciation; the endeavors on pain without anyone's sympathy for one's own failure. It was just a way of life to accept the unexpected surprises in man.

I needed to fully justify myself for my own curiosity in an endless path of reaching the top of a mountain in Southeast Asia. I grew up there and had to face the actualization of struggle. Years ago it was unthinkable to acknowledge that martial arts training was relentlessly crude, extremely harsh and caused pain. Students didn't think about their feelings. They had faith that pain was part of their training experience. The older generation of men that went before me had a much tougher life in practice.

Practicing and enhancing the moods of passion, which fully involved training in Hakka Kun Tao or silat, made me over the years a more conscience-minded individual in understanding others with better comprehension. Years of training had a lasting effect on my behavior in thinking, working, playing and in my moods coming from my senses. It made me a better established leader in practice.

From the very beginning, when I started the learning process of martial arts, I understood that the martial arts practice stood for more than just punching and kicking. The complexity involving the practice alone was an enhanced adventure to reality; when failure became a conscious mental obstacle to overcome.

No one, even at his good behavior or even the best well-trained master of martial arts, escapes a reality check for uncontrollable anguish at times. At nature's best it is expected for human beings to strive harder to fulfill their destiny toward perfection. Impartial to martial torture is reaching the top without accidents. Most mountain climbers are successful at reaching their objectives, but not without some failed efforts due to costly ignorance. It relates to life in general, in business and everything else with the exception of mountain climbing and flying planes. Human ignorance becomes a tragedy!

During my studies of martial arts, learning to understand the quality in harmony and to accept life for what it is, was quite a hard learned experience. Any duration in lengthy endeavors for the painstaking events of physical torture is habit forming and with the end never being in sight of one's point of view. Every practice in training becomes one man's frustration and also one man's alliance. Striving for perfection could be considered the ultimate goal! For me, it was a must of getting somewhere. To live healthy and prosperously enjoying a spiritual art in which the mind, body and soul harmoniously transmit themselves to wisdom of ages. In a sense, a serene quality of life is like a shadow that follows a silhouette that remains calm and tranquil.

It was out of necessity that I overcame my unexpected failures by learning the truth and consequences and consider those a learning tool for success. If what could be wrong today, it was the absolutes of tomorrow's clearness for better ideas. The teachers of the past, through my recollections, were less informed and leaned more toward the idea of philosophically transitioning to a spiritual life of understanding the elements of nature. They held onto the belief of an everlasting life and unification in which soul, nature and universe blend together as a remarkable idea. With their philosophical thinking of spirituality as being one with the Earth, they kept forgetting that physical pain was hard and had to be endured by the student of their choosing. Therefore they could not comprehend how to deal with a student that had to go through any perceivably painstaking event. Students often became poor, disoriented souls, and some even died during practice. In today's world, things are totally different. Masters or teachers have lots of sources to gain information and are able to create health beneficiary programs for the public. They carefully plan curriculums to run productive schools. With more knowledge they become far better teachers in coaching groups of people.

I continue my writing, like beginning this episode by reminiscing eventful memories of my past together with some historical moments. After some crucial years of experiencing imprisonment, first by the Japanese from 1942–1945, then by the Indonesian freedom fighters who took control over the Dutch East Indies when Indonesia declared its independence from Dutch rule.

Many of the Dutch Indonesians were kept in different internment camps. Most internees were women, children and teenage boys. It became apparent that their situation would worsen, especially the treatment of Indonesian youth who hated the Dutch. There were several prisoner of war camps. In Java alone, there were four camps – Bandung, Surabaya, Semarang and Djakarta – with others scattered around Sumatra, Celebes and Borneo. Some captured allied soldiers received severe physical torture when caught escaping any of the camps. A few were immediately executed and others were found decapitated.

As part of the generation of Dutch Indonesian men (perhaps the last) that grew up during the Dutch colonial times, it is hard to imagine that our children and grandchildren, who grew up in a Western world, have no understanding of what it feels like to be a free soul and to live in a land of milk and honey and a free enterprise system like the United States.

Beyond their reach, as far as their thinking capabilities will ever be able to grace their souls with understanding, perhaps someday they can come to comprehend what the elderly had to overcome and how they paved the way for them to live free and create their own luck for a better future. None of the younger generation of Dutch Indonesians, and the generation of baby boomers before them, has ever had to experience the tragedy and misfortunes of war that we experienced some 67 years ago.

During the years 1942–1946, an era I still remember, I was six years old. I was taken from my family and put into an internment camp by the Japanese occupational forces. My mother and brothers were put into another camp. The Kempai Tai, or Japanese Gestapo, had tortured many of us for no reason except to satisfy their sadism. Several of the men, women and children in the camp had been stricken with severe tropical diseases – malaria and berry berry. Berry berry was caused by a great lack of vitamins and being exhausted and undernourished. Anyone stricken with the disease was immobilized and became so bloated that the weight of unwanted fat and liquids that they couldn't move finger.

As my mind dwells on historical events, I would like to recollect these moments in times. I already explained in my first book about the camp conditions. Referred to as the Iron Bar Hotel in the camp we were in, it had several torture chambers. Prior to the invasion, Dutch and American corporations used the bungalows as vacation centers for their staff and their families.

The Japanese were full of hatred toward other races and especially retaliated against the downed Allied pilots when any were captured and brought to the Iron Bar Hotel. Under those circumstances, I grew to adulthood quickly.

Realism came from graduating from the school of hard knocks came early to me, and I think the Great Divine or God for the experience alone. While growing up, I had to overcome many obstacles that I faced alone, while comforting others in their need to cross their paths of spiritual hardship.

My father was a Dutch Colonial prisoner of war and was captured and sent to work on the Burma Railroad tracks like many others. Many Allied soldiers died on those tracks. Each railroad tie laid was a dead Allied soldier's body. Most of the captured Allies were British, American, Dutch, Dutch Indonesian, Australian and East Indian. Planned as a military intent for the invasion of India, Japanese military leaders planned to build a railroad track from Burma into India and, as time progressed, they would join forces with the Germans to seize the Suez Canal and Egypt. The construction of the infamous Burma Railroad was a tragedy in terms of the cost of human life. Most of the Allies died of starvation, berry berry, malaria or exhaustion.

At the start, the Allied Troops fighting in the Burmese and Rangoon military campaigns were comprised of British, Indian, Ghurka, American, Dutch, French, Australian, New Zealand and Chinese under the American military generals Stillwell and Wingate. The Allied Forces were under the command of British Lord Mountbatten with Wingate as the deputy commander. As a fighting force, the Allied Troops were faced with internal problems. They were short of medical supplies, and plagued by illness and monsoons.

When the War fell in the Allies' favor by mid-1943, Japanese military leaders were still convinced that Japan had superiority in forces and in overall strength. The Japanese underestimated the will of the American people and its industrial might, the US increased production of war material for building ships and aircraft.

Sooner than expected and to the overwhelming surprise of Japanese military leaders, the American war effort and the Allied troops had plenty of provisions and equipment to chase the Japanese. Japanese military forces were almost out of supplies. American submarines and surface ships were able to sink most of their tankers and cargo vessels.

Without their much-needed supplies, it became even more crucial and drastic for the fighting forces of Imperial Japan. Japan was nearly brought to its knees by the Allies. Still too stubborn to give up, the Japanese military forces continued to fight and kept fighting in hopes they would regain their land losses in territories taken by the Allied Expeditionary Forces in the jungles of Burma and Rangoon.

The turning tide of the Burma military campaign highly favored the Allies when the Derby Rangers, Muriel Marauders and various Allied military units were constantly on the attack, and they overran Japanese supply depots and military bases. In June, 1944 General LeMay was put in charge as the Air Commander over the US Army Air Force in Southeast Asia. Together with other Allied air units, they stepped up their bombing raids in Burma, Rangoon, Thailand, Borneo, Tuck Island, Tokyo and other Japanese naval bases throughout the rim of the Southwest Pacific and destroyed most of their objectives.

The constant bombing raids over Japan's held territories in Southeast Asia had devastating effects. There was mass destruction to the Japanese Army, air and sea forces.

In retaliation for Japan's infamous attack on Pearl Harbor on December 7, 1941, America was punishing the sons of The Rising Sun. US Naval Warships, submarines and fighter planes on aircraft sank. Together with the Allies, Japan's pride for their mastery of the skies and lands was totally broken by America's assault against the Japanese. The American people repaid Imperial Japan 100 times over for what they did with the air raid on the Hawaiian Islands. When Japan attacked the US Naval Base at Pearl Harbor on December 7, 1941, they attacked the entire United States. The Japanese naval commanders made a crucial and military blunder by not following up their aggressive action. All of America's carrier force comprised of four aircraft carriers when to sea during the attack on Pearl Harbor and gave America the chance to strike back. What most never realized was that the nature of the American people was always built on unity and strength. As the first chapter for my second book, I would like to share some of my studies in World History and also recall some of those events I was able to live through, with my comprehension of the past that will follow me into the future.

Slowly the combined Allied Forces advaned into Japanese held territories in the Malay peninsula. After General LeMay stepped up the Allied bombing raids and sea barrage, 60 supply and warships went down to the ocean floor. The Island of Tuck was one of Japan's largest war depots and military bases. This brought the strength and might of the Japanese air, land and sea forces to a drastic end in the Southwest Pacific.

At the same time, Dutch and U.S. warships were able to repay the Japanese navy for the loss of a whole Allied fleet in the Java Sea. On May 27, 1942, one of the largest sea battles was held between a small Allied naval force comprised of Dutch, American, English and Australian vessels. The opposing side was comprised of a far larger Japanese naval armada with an overwhelming strike force of aircraft carriers, battle wagons, heavy cruisers, light-heavy cruisers and 80 destroyers and submarines. The Allied naval sea force had only 16 outdated warships under the command of Dutch Rear Admiral Karel Doorman. Most of the Allied ships went down in the Bandung Strait with the exception of two crippled Dutch destroyers and a heavily damaged American destroyer. These ships managed to steam into the Port of Sydney in Australia. After being repaired, those ships and their crew fought against the warships of the Japanese navy.

The Japanese land forces lost 100,000 men in Burma, Rangoon and French Indochina. Many Japanese soldiers died of starvation or the lack of medical supplies and arms. Most of those men fighting the Allies were also young men and just as inexperienced as the Allied forces in that part of the Southwest Pacific. The greatest setback the Japanese military leaders faced was the loss of the forces' will to fight as the tide began to turn against them. Roadsides were littered with the rotting bodies of Japanese soldiers left as the Japanese army retreated while the refreshed Allied troops advanced and began to recapture Japanese held territories. The smell of rotting corpses was so bad that Allied soldiers kept towels wrapped around their faces to keep them from fainting from the smell. After the British military forces liberated the Dutch Indonesians from Indonesian internment camps, they put us on a British destroyer for our own safety. We took the HMS Glenn Royal to Singapore. Finally I was starting to realize how immensely grateful I was for the heroic efforts of the British Parachute Units for liberating us from the concentration camps. Those men, with their red and green berets, were not only great warriors but also fearless men of steel. Against an overwhelming force of Japanese and Indonesian troops and militias, the British regimental parachute units were dropped into our camp and surprised the guards. They had to fight their way out and brought us to an Allied military camp in the harbor of Surabaya. Some of the British paratroopers were wounded or killed, and I will always treasure and honor them for their unselfish sacrifices for us.

The British Special Forces units and the units of the Gurkha 10th Rifle Regiment fought bitterly against the Indonesian militias and some Japanese military units, who continued to fight the Allies. For them the War was never finished. In the Java campaign alone, British Indian Armed Forces lost almost a division of battle hardened troops on the outskirts of the city of Surabaya in East Java. They were under attack from Indonesian civilians, militias and Dutch trained Indonesian troops. The battle in the city cost British Indian General Melaby his life. While the General was negotiating a peace treaty with Indonesian officials, an Indonesian sniper shot him. Hours after the failed attempt for a peaceful solution the RAF launched a full scale air raid killing thousands of civilians. It was a British reprisal for killing one of their generals.

When we, the two hundred internees, arrived in Singapore, we were brought to a British receiving camp. I was transferred to another camp with five other boys in my group to the "Irene" camp named after a Dutch princess. My friends and I were placed in a bungalow with some adults to supervise us. There was a native Malaysian cook assigned to our group to prepare our meals. What was most shocking to us while living in the bungalow was that we were free and living under completely different circumstances, not unlike the clouds passing above us. Something we had not dreamed about was the chance to be independent. Life was full of miracles for me as a malnourished boy of 10. The British officers managing the camp were under a British Colonel in charge of hundreds of evacuees. They kept us busy with all sorts of sports, mainly soccer, before the classrooms for the school were built. Sick women, children and older men received special health treatment from Dutch, English and American physicians for tropical swears, malaria, cholera and stomach ailments.

We stayed productive and physically active under the British officers, and there was no idle time. Some of the boys received good training in the fighting art of pugilism under controlled supervision. We had protective gear for boxing. Our hands were bandaged with pieces of cloth and we worked the inside leather jackets of old helmets for head gear and a rubber mouth piece. Most of the boys enjoyed the atmosphere that was kept outside the camp and in the jungle of Malaysia. The boys went ape for the art of fighting. One thing about each of the British military officers, they knew what young boys needed most was strong physical activities to keep the mind and body well motivated and occupied.

A young British lieutenant, a paratrooper, was assigned to me. He attended my practice sessions in running since he felt this is what I needed most to regain my strength. I participated in most of the activities, like boxing, running and soccer. I felt stronger each day as time moved on, and the young lieutenant was actually my guardian and gave me another assignment as a food and beverage distributor for the evacuees in the camp. It was a very likable job to assist others at my mature age of 10. I will never forget the young British lieutenant who was like an older brother and taught me many social skills.

Through his wisdom and field experiences, the most I could say as to what he taught was to be punctual and to uphold your responsibility to others as you hold your responsibility to yourself. He knew me inside and out. I was full of hatred toward the Japanese and had a very bitter and negative disposition. Looking back at his teachings and in what it did to me, I can easily see the value of freedom of spirit and what it meant for the Indonesian people to be a free nation. I was the same when a young British lieutenant took me under his wing.

The best thing I remember was a most interesting occasion that I was very privileged to experience. The young lieutenant had a pleasant conversation with me as we were both sitting under coconut trees in the jungle outside our camp. The young Englishman was more like a brother and spiritual guide to me and I had never met anyone like him. "William," the lieutenant started our conversation, "what is it that you expect out of life?"

I replied, "I honestly don't know, Sir."

He continued by explaining to me, "I fought most of my physical battles, lost lots of friends and think the War is now over for me. My concern is you, deep inside you, as I sensed, you are still fighting a hated spirited battle with demons. I fully understand in what you had to live through, but at the same time William, you need to let go. There is still so much to live for. You are so young and yet, there will always be many issues in life. Always remember me. Train to live, eat to live and the more you train, the more you keep your mind, body and spirit healthy and young!"

I said to him, "Thank you lieutenant for your advice and everything else you taught me. I shall always treasure you as my guardian angel for the rest of my life."

He looked at me, smiled, and then told me, "Tomorrow things will be different. The camp will be given back to the Dutch and I am going home to England. It was great to have worked with you and please, take care."

Always with a grand smile and handsome face, he shook my hand and with a friendly tap on my shoulder he walked off toward the officers' quarters. I felt some tears rolling through my eye lids as I looked at the young British lieutenant walking away, proud, strong and very upright, like a British paratrooper at a military speed. That was the last time I saw him.

First we had to sit idle in the camp, after a Dutch lieutenant colonel took over. All had to be examined by Dutch, English and American doctors. As soon as the Dutch had control, most of the sports activities were abandoned and we had to go to school. Our vacation was over and the British officers were gone. In their place came Dutch military officers and soldiers. Life then became, in my opinion, very dull. The food was as good as could be expected. The food they fed us was below our expectations, but it was okay. We managed to enjoy our lunch and dinners. Some of the boys had to go to the camp clinic for upset stomachs. They overate on cabbage and powdered eggs.

Under Dutch supervision everything had to be punctual. The educational classes the Dutch provided for us were inadequate. The school lacked supplies, books, paper and pencils. The classrooms were overcrowded and each teacher had 60 to 70 kids. Under the circumstances, learning was impractical due to the hectic situation. Students were a mixture of first graders through high school students.

Under the Dutch, things were different from the British. With the Brits, boys could still be boys and were allowed a freer hand of playing in the forest outside of camp. We played war games with downed Japanese Zero fighters. Some of the dive bombers that were shot down still had machine guns behind the pilot's seat. We saw the Dutch military officers parading up and down the corridors like straight marching broomsticks and walking clocks, and they always wanted the last word above all the miseries of life. When it came to food, we preferred American, British and Dutch food in that order.

Some of us became very sick from the heavy, fattening foods provided by the Dutch kitchen. What we needed most were hot peppers instead of margarine sticks. In some ways I felt sorry for the Dutch cooks. They lacked understanding of the intake of natural vitamins by the Southwest Pacific Islanders, which we belonged to as a race of people.

When I look back at the war years at stories I can share with friends, one strikes me as most profound. A Dutch cook was going to treat us to a spaghetti dinner and had all the ingredients to make his pasta sauce. What they gave him was Chinese egg noodles for his Italian dish. Most of the evacuees were quite happy with the imitation of spaghetti and regretted later on that they had eaten the Chinese noodles since they did not taste like real spaghetti. I left the dinner table and excused myself. I snuck out to an American military unit that was posted only a mile away from our camp. I became acquainted with some of the soldiers during my playtime in the jungle. The Americans invited me to join them for dinner. I enjoyed the American food much better. We had chicken noodle soup, French fries, meatballs and ice cream for dessert.

Schooling on plantations was only for children of staff employees. The schools were funded by several different corporations and children of those employees could get an education to finish elementary school at a plantation school. To broaden their knowledge in education, the children had to go to larger cities to finish high school, college or university. The parents had to find a boarding school or places where their sons or daughters could stay and maintain their schooling under the supervisory guidance of others. The cost of education was tremendous. It was a costly undertaking for parents to send their teenage children to Europe for more advanced education.

When I ended up in a school desk for the first time, I felt terribly confused and became scared of the boy I shared my desk with. He was a 16-year-old teenager and almost finished with high school. I was totally lost in this world, being in school. I had no books and nothing to write on. To make it worse, I was absolutely illiterate and had never been to school. At age 10 and not knowing how to read or write, I felt stupid! There was hardly a space to breathe in an overcrowded classroom with all the lively kids that were continuously being energized.

Some fights broke out between stronger and bigger boys. Whatever reasons they had, they were interesting for me to watch. For a boy that enjoys the painstaking event of a good fight, I liked the energy the two boys had displayed in action. There was their grappling, punching, kicking and fighting skills through their natural ability.

After the excitement of the day in the classroom, two Dutch teachers finally arrived and broke up the spiritual and physical engagement of two healthy boys that just could not sit still. One of the boys, a certain Hendriks, became my hero for his combative method of fighting. He was a street fighter. The teachers were in for lots of surprises. They came directly from Holland and were shocked by the environment in which they had to educate kids. It was hard for them, not knowing where to even start creating their curriculum to educate students – in mixed classes without appropriate books and supplies. The start for the teachers from Holland was, perhaps, the hardest time they had to face. Their motherland was in a stage of rebuilding their own country from war, and now, here they were in the tropics with unexpected surprises.

The teenage boy sitting beside me was as uncomfortable as I was. When the teacher came by our desk to explain something to him, it confused me a lot because I didn't know who the teacher was teaching. A couple of weeks later, books and supplies finally arrived from Holland and London. Things started to get back to normal, and I was able in a short time to make it to the second grade with the speed classes provided by the Dutch school system.

For having lived by myself in a British Receiving Center, I became totally reliant on myself and was very independent from others. I had practically raised myself the last six years and had a hard time coping with someone looking over my shoulder. A Dutch reunion organization for the reunification of families brought my mother, brother and me together in Singapore. I was overjoyed. I knew in my heart how I had missed my mother and brothers during our years of separation. It felt kind of strange to suddenly see my mom back and by brothers giving each other lip service for doing the wrong thing. Strange as it may seem, I always missed the healthy fights we brothers had in the de Thouars family.

The most important man in our family was my dad, and we were uncertain of his existence and where he was. We gained out of gathered information from the Dutch military that he was a prisoner of war in Thailand. Half of the boys in camp were reunited with their families after years of separation. One morning a Dutch man came by the house we were living in and informed us to be ready in 24 hours to be flown to Bangkok, Siam for a reunion with my father. The man was a public servant of the Dutch Embassy in Singapore and made arrangements with the civilian air transport of the RAF. We were on the list, and the flight from Singapore to Bangkok was quite an experience for me since I'd never flown before. Due to the shortage of qualified pilots to fly civilian aircraft, our pilot had to serve one year longer and was assigned the job of transporting refugees to designated places.

The story the man told us was significant to me. It was his DC3 together with another group in his air wing that was comprised of similar airplanes that had dropped the British parachute units together with units of the Gurkha special forces in our camp to liberate us! I could not even imagine how I was able to tell my grandchildren my story, and about the paratroopers in the same plane where I was sitting and about those brave men who gave their lives to make this world free from oppression. How mothers back in England and elsewhere in the world had to shed tears for their loss of their most treasured possession, the loss of their sons. It was just as my mother had when my oldest brother Henry was killed by a sniper where he stood guard. Henry served in the Royal Dutch Colonial Army and was attached to the 10th Motor Battalion.

* * *

This sketch is the HMS Glenn Royal (formerly HMS Glenn Royd) seen steaming away off the coast of Java with 200 Dutch and Dutch Indonesian evacuees aboard. This warship could easily be considered a light-heavy cruiser and was later commissioned as a heavy escort cruiser. Her displacement in armament comprised four 9-inch guns, six howitzers, heavy automatic machine guns and 50mm anti-aircraft guns. Per-square tonnage, the ship weighs 17,000 metric tons and could crank 50 land miles per hour in speed. In addition, the Glenn Royd also had two torpedo tubes on each to launch attacks on adversaries at sea. This fully equipped war vessel was a fierce participant in the Southwest Pacific Theater and, with a crew of 200, annihilated civilian and Japanese naval vessels. It also sunk five Japanese submarines to the ocean floor with her depth charges.

PART 2
TORN BETWEEN TWO WORLDS

To a point in my philosophical thinking, I try not to bring up political events in our world structure. But I can't help also recollecting the circumstances in which I grew up. How I saw world events 66 years ago and to the most recent time, it has been all about economics, welfare and wealth. Poverty has always been a disease that has stricken mankind like a pestilence and, like a disease, it spreads all over. In a social standing it is most unfortunate that the rich get richer and the poor get poorer. The rich do well and make money off the poor!

Taking into consideration that after World War II, the growth of insurance companies and the drug industry had a greater expansion of progress in the world and, at the same time, the social welfare system was brought to a level that some people became extremely rich or extremely poor. As an individual who survived times of war and economic disasters, this is the reason for mentioning the evens of the world. As I grew up, I was a surviving soul in the asphalt jungle like so many of my generation.

Amazingly, as time evolved through thousands of episodes, in each man's life develops an evolution that through a differentiation of one's far sided thinking man had formed a higher level; of foreseeing progress. Our history in events can never be taken for granted. It was like a revolving door to our future. Without any form of history, our future would be non-existent. In a changing world, we, as individuals, look toward a process of unlimited resources and to an essence of hope and in hope we find a remedy in which we are able to meet tomorrow's challenges. Consider the future as an unknown world. It is a phase in which things are moving so fast that mankind has the tendency to become clustered in the lust for greed. Literally the human race was, in a sense, always destined to rule the Earth and harvested politics and created corruption. Any man or woman who loves to venture through a resourceful source that will lead them to a prosperous future.

Mankind has always ventured in the building of cultures. The drawback that many older cultures are facing is that, recessively, they have the tendency to stop progress by keeping people illiterate. Every government in any of those countries that are considered Third World

Countries, like those in South America, the Middle East and Southeast Asia, kept their populations down from reaching an ultimate goal for a good welfare system. Good welfare is created through good business practices. This seemed greatly lacking in the hands of the politicians that run those underprivileged countries. They have had to rely on social and economic aid of better suited lands that have adequate economic structure in their social welfare system.

Prosperous nations that lead the rest of the world like the U.S., Japan, China, India, Great Britain, Scandinavia, Europe and Russia are working together to bail out the less fortunate nations. What is affecting the peace treaty and economic recoveries in the Third World Countries relates mostly to the unstable governing bodies. Constant friction among the Eastern religious leaders and infighting among different terrorists groups has created threats worldwide. The greatest world threat right now is between Pakistan and India. As a result, the United Nations, led by the US, has had to interfere with military forces to control the unrest-stricken countries like Iraq, Afghanistan and also in the Middle East. After WWII, the situation in the Far East and Middle East had never changed; it only emerged to a far greater margin that caused the stronger countries a staggering loss of their economic resources. In some ways, we all have been influenced by man's nature for greed.

Through my simple knowledge of the world of socialism in the 20th and 21st centuries, I became fully aware of many things that always were there in good times and bad. They influenced my wordy description of my written text. During the course of experiencing those drastic moments in life over the years, they have made me a better established individual. I overcame many obstacles and had to witness some of life's hectic events. I also listened to the actual stories of others as they were relating them to me.

Without them, the individuals involved, it would be impossible for me to write anything down. Deeply as it always had concerned me for the individual who shared with me their richly endeavored happenings in their past, my gratitude is expressed. It saddens me that a few of my friends had long ago folded their hands – some through illness and some through natural causes. I shall always treasure my friends forever because, in essence, their presence has never left my soul!

My story started when Holland gave back her colonies to the island nation of Indonesia in 1950. During that time, when power was transferred from the Dutch Colonial government to the Indonesian leaders, the situation over the length of the Indonesian islands caused chaos for the Dutch Indonesians and Europeans. When the Dutch withdrew all her Armed Forces out of the archipelago and brought their military men and their families back to Holland, they left behind a few military units to help build and reconstruct the Indonesian Armed Forces into an adequate military defensive fighting force.

Suddenly the Dutch nation became totally overwhelmed with an overflow of 100,000 service men and their families. This small country in the Netherlands was already suffering a great shortage of housing and was running low on food supplies. Holland was still in a rebuilding stage after WWII. Adding to the staggering numbers of military personnel returning to Holland, the Dutch government was also demobilizing the Dutch Colonial Army, the KNIL, and ended up with another 25,000 of Holland's most loyal fighting forces and their families returning home. The Colonial Army had served the Dutch for 350 years when it disbanded in 1950. Several of the high ranking officers in the KNIL and a few other Army units joined the Indonesian military and trained the Armed Forces in Holland's former colonies to create a greater military force in Southeast Asia.

Many historical events occurred in 1950, during the transition of power, when several political parties wanted to separate from the Republic of Indonesia for their own independence. Civil unrest among the party leaders brought economic devastation to the island nation. Several guerilla groups formed as the situation in the islands spun out of control. For none other than their own political reasons, they started to furiously attack the Indonesian military convoys or guerilla fighters of the opposition party. The worst of the guerilla fighters were members of the Darul Islam (Islamic Group) or the Barisan Sakit Hati (Specific Group for Justice). These two groups had always been feared by the native Indonesians who lived in villages and in small towns. Most of the bitter fighting was done in the jungle of West Java between the Indonesian Arm and the guerillas. The rebellious fighters constantly ambushed military trucks or the cars of employees from nearby plantations or factories.

Rebellious youth in larger cities, like Djakarta, Semarang and Surabaya, were greatly encouraged after watching gangster movies starring Humphrey Bogart and George Raft. They began to develop their own street gangs and nothing was sacred to them anymore. Those street gangs attacked innocent people during daylight hours or at night. Small businesses, restaurants or little stores were constantly being robbed. The gang members took firearms from old Dutch military depots and bought off the guards guarding the buildings.

The city police were incapable of handling the ongoing pressure and the situation in their cities for quite a while was prolonged. The gang members eventually turned their activities to brutal killing and terrorism. Daily shootouts between City Police and the killing of innocent victims were led to an even greater extent by groups of youth who were led by corrupted officials.

Among Indonesians, Dutch Indonesians or Dutch was an uneasy feeling to walk the city streets without protection. During a day of civil unrest in Surabaya in East Java, I once witnessed a would-be robber, a youthful man with a hand gun, being punished by an old postal clerk. The postal clerk was minding his own business when the would be robber jumped the counter and began yelling at the postal clerk and his fellow workers. The young man was screaming loudly – his voice could be heard for quite a distance. The old postal clerk jumped out of his chair and landed elbow strikes and butts in the rib cage of the attacking robber. With an extreme fist of fury coming from the hands of the old postal clerk, he landed a forceful blow on the head of the young robber sending the assailant flat on the floor and into dreamland. Not long after the Indonesian Military Police arrived at the post office and dragged the lifeless body of the robber outside into an awaiting Jeep. The man in charge of the Indonesian Military Police Unit was the son of the postal clerk who happened to be an old-school Pentjak Silat player.

Like revolving occurrences in any war torn country, the circumstances brought challegnes to Indonesia's progress for unity in the early 1950s. It was a difficult time for the Indonesian government to bring the provinces together as one nation. What was happening in those early years was that several high-ranking Dutch military officers were in disagreement with Indonesia's regime. They were planning a military coup to retake two cities in West Java, Bandung and the capital city of Djakarta.

The former Dutch Captain Raymond Westerling had organized and drafted a small volunteer army comprised of former members of his parachute commando units. All the men who volunteer for Westerling's command unit once served under his command while he was in charge of the Royal Dutch Para-Commando Brigade. These men were loyal to the Dutch Captain and followed his well-planned coup in the city of Bandung. But they failed in the capital city due to interference by Dutch military leaders who were against the takeover. The fall of Bandung was accomplished without stiff resistance from the Indonesian troops who occupied the city. They were totally surprised by the strategic military attack of the Dutch Captain. Small units of his Para–Commandos overran the weapon depots first and moved with lightening speed to capture the city within hours.

Captain Raymond Westerling was a hardened veteran of World War II and had also served as an officer with the British Special Forces. He received his British military training first in Scotland and later in Canada. He was assigned to a group of military specialists in jungle warfare for the Burma Campaign. As a front soldier, Raymond Westerling fought on several fronts and gained rank to Captain. Adding to his repertoire were the war fronts of Burma, Africa and Southeast Asian peninsula. The Captain led several commando raids against Japanese military objectives and in the oil fields of Borneo. His main objective was to destroy and clear out Japanese military radar stations and supply depots with very small military units under his command.

In 1944 while in Serawak, West Borneo, the Captain sustained wounds from a 50mm machine gun manned by a Japanese machine gun unit. His men brought him to safety to an Allied military hospital in Rangoon. After his recovery, the British Command Center referred Westerling back to the Dutch Military Headquarters in Burma since the Captain was also serving with the Dutch Army. The Dutch military staff, under whose command he had served, ordered Westerling to parachute into the jungle of Sumatra alone. He had to seek out and form a special forces team comprised of military units of the colonial army that were scattered around the city of Palembang. After struggling through the rough jungle terrain, Westerling finally came to the city and was stricken with malaria. Immediately, despite his malaria, he went through with his plan and formed and trained the Royal Dutch Special Forces Brigade. From 1946 until 1949, the Captain and his Special Forces Team paved the way for other Dutch military forces to capture all the islands back in the West Indies.

Westerling was a soldier first and an organizer second. With his military strategy and leadership, he was able to organize several units of chosen military men that now comprised members of the Dutch Colonial Army. Now as a Dutch Captain, he, together with his newly formed Dutch Para-Commandos, seized the whole island of Sumatra and retook several other islands in the Dutch East Indies. At the time, his smaller brigade of Para-Commandos had a greater advantage in the less organized and inexperienced armies. He kept the city of Bandung under his military control until the day he was ordered to surrender with his troops by the Dutch General Buurman Van Vreden. Many of the men serving under Westerling that had been participants in the coup were later imprisoned by the Indonesian Military on the Island of "Unrest," off the coast of Djakarta. The hardest part for the Indonesian Military Officers was sending those men to the imprisonment camp. Some of these officers had also served under Westerling in the Colonial Army and he had led these men to action. The Dutch Officers who cooperated with the Captain had to serve their time in Dutch Military Prisons in Holland. As for the Captain, he had tried to escape the Indonesian authorities and was captured by the British in Singapore. After several months in captivity, the Dutch and British Military Tribunal dismissed the case and Westerling left as a free man and later became a successful opera singer in Belgium and Holland.

Two years later, after the military coup of the Dutch Captain in 1950 came to the surface, another high ranking former Dutch military Colonial Army Officer, a certain Andy Abdul Azis who had been stationed in the city of Macassar on the island of Celebes, was in the spotlight. Colonel Azis was in command of all the Indonesian troops in the city. The ex-Colonel was disenchanted and bitterly opposed to the policies of the new Indonesian Republic. Bitter fighting between the internal groups of Indonesian Armed Forces was soon unleashed. One group supported Azis, and the other group fought against the military units of the former Colonel, which forced members of the Dutch Colonial Army to remain in their military base. The Colonial Army was surrounded by the two forces fighting each other. Soldiers serving in the Colonial Army were ordered to only retaliate when they were overrun or attacked by opposing forces. After two weeks of intense fighting between the two Indonesian military forces, the Netherlands had to intervene in order to keep the peace. The Royal Dutch

Navy first sent a destroyer, The Evertsen, into the harbor of Maccassar and started to bombard the city with heavy gun fire. The two military forces were heavily shelled and many of their men were killed. After several hours, the naval salvos became so intense that both sides gave up fighting and peace was restored to the city. The action of the Dutch was mostly meant to protect the encircled Dutch Colonial Army and their families. A week after the halt of military actions, a Dutch light-heavy cruiser and two destroyers dropped anchor off the coast of Macassar. A Dutch cargo ship later steamed into the harbor of Maccassar and embarked all remaining members of the Dutch Colonial Army and their families and returned them to Holland. Colonel Andy Abdul Azis surrendered to the Indonesian authorities and was later beheaded in Djakarta.

Any further Indonesian military actions against rebellious uprisings took place in 1953 in South Moluccas. Led by the Indonesian Colonel Kawilarang, an ex-Dutch Colonial Army Officer, military forces landed on the coast of Amboina to shut down Dr. Samukil's rebellious military forces, who rebelled against the Indonesian regime. Dr. Samukil's troops were mostly men who had served under the Dutch Captain Westerling and fought a fierce battle against the Indonesian landing forces. Both sides, the rebels in the South Molluccas and the Indonesian troops in Serang and Amboina, suffered many deaths and heavy casualties during exchange of fire. With an overwhelming military force comprised of better trained troops and more adequate language and equipment, the Indonesian landing forces were finally able to shut down the aggression of Dr. Samukil and his rebels after months of bitter fighting.

Under the circumstances, it was hard for half breeds, or Dutch Indonesians like me, to remain in the land of my birth. Most of us had to hold back our anger or frustration even if it was in defense of oneself. The hatred against the Dutch from the Indonesian natives was intensified. The pure Dutch in Holland refused to accept us as Dutch equals. To them, we were intruders and beggars who would plunder our Motherland, Holland.

Grief stricken as I was with the situation and not knowing what else to do, I went to live in Bandung, West Java. After residing for a while in that city, I contacted the Dutch Consul General and wanted to know if I had any chance of repatriating to Holland as a Dutch citizen. After all I had been through, I felt I was still a man without a

The RAF De 3 that flew us to Bangkok from Singapore

She "would be roller blading surprised by a postal clerk with pentjac silat.

country. I thought to myself to hell with the queen, to hell with Holland and to hell with the rest of the world. In my way of thinking, I was really happy for my older brother Maurice who had signed up with the van Heutz battalion to fight in Korea. He and his battalion were part of the United Nations Police Force, and their job was defending the South from the North. Even then, when there was a possibility of war, it was much better than the circumstances I lived in. I was not blaming anyone else for my situation. There were many other individuals in the same boat as I. Here I was very unsure of my future and stuck in a city where I felt unwanted. For that reason, I hated politics and governments for playing Russian roulette with peoples' lives. I was 16 years old at the time. My plea to go to Holland was denied.

The only good thing I got out of living in the city of Bandung was the martial arts training I received from an uncle, a certain Edward de Vries who was my mother's cousin. Uncle Eddy was an ardent and experienced practitioner of Pentjak Silat and played various native fighting arts. The typical fighting styles Uncle Eddy participated in were the usual combative arts from West Java, for instance Serak the family style, Ci Mane and Kemango Ulut. My uncle was a very quiet man, a gentleman that allowed me to live with him. He was also a true, hardened Colonial soldier. During the uprising at Atjeh in Sumatra, he had to combat the Atjeh warriors who were attacking the Dutch. He also fought as an Allied soldier against the Japanese in Burma. As a teacher Uncle Eddy was harsh, unmerciful and relentless. As his nephew, I was in for more physical abuse.

Thinking back on those days, I actually enjoyed the hard training and severe painstaking events. It taught me a lot about a practical teacher that could not share any philosophical thinking. What my uncle taught me will always be an essence as part of nature in me for surviving. By remembering him, I also followed in his footsteps by physically and tortuously teaching others who came to learn from me. Most of my students came in, not for one lesson, but for the duration of physical endurance in pain.

I felt very uncomfortable after living with my uncle in Bandung for months and not having a job to support him and to pay my rent. It was never in my nature to mooch off someone and to get everything for free. I understood from the beginning that a man has to work and needs to be very enterprising for his own progression to success. I decided to ask the advice of an experienced older Dutch Indonesian man, a friend of my father, about my situation and Indonesia's future. I had long and lengthy conversations full of hope with my father's friend. He advised me to find a place in Djakarta and eventually try to escape aboard an Italian ship to Europe when I had the chance. The Italian shipping lines had more ships going to Indonesia in the 1950s. Many Dutch Indonesians found not only refuge aboard Italian vessels, but also passage on wonderful passenger boats.

A few weeks later, I found my chance to move to Djakarta, the capital city, and I was able to find a home in the city's worse slammed area in Glodok, a suburb filled with millions and millions of people. Glodok, as a district, had always been the most poverty stricken place. As a resident it was sometimes scary, and one was always forced to be on guard for the unexpected surprises when walking the streets. The neighborhood where I lived was full of horrific nightmares ranging from street killers, thieves and ill-fated prostitutes. How interesting it was for me to see these street folks living on street corners and, from my observation, always stalking victims. Much to my luck in life, I was always able to evade getting involved with unwanted characters. I knew they were always bad news for an innocent soul or victim of society.

One morning I was on my way to the harbor trying to find a job as a brick shorter, one who stacks bricks for construction crews, as my way of escape from Indonesia. While taking a city tram that morning and during my walk to the harbor, I noticed eight guys stalking and following me from a distance. I thought to myself, "Here I am a skinny teenager against eight guys. I'm in a terrible position. Where can I escape? I know no one." First I walked a slow pace, and then I quickly changed to a faster speed since I was hoping to get rid of the guys following me. Coming to an intersection, I had to walk through a back alley. Then I started to run for dear life. With the eight men closing in on me I found that the faster I ran, the faster they followed me.

I was so hasty in running away that I made a big mistake when I took a wrong turn in the back alley and stumbled against an eight-foot high retaining wall that closed off the alley. I was standing opposite from the direction that would have led me to the harbor. The surface on the top of the wall was cemented with broken glass, and for having lived a mostly dangerous life during its short existence, I immediately knew that I had to think quickly to escape my followers.

When the men closed in on me, I saw a large, wooden construction pin lying near a garbage dumpster, just a few feet from where I was standing. I dove to the pin and with lightening speed drove the piece of wood deep in the stomach of the largest man of the bunch. With agility I did not know I had, I made a desperate leap with my springy legs and could touch the surface of the wall. In that moment that I had been waiting for, I went over the side and ran faster toward the harbor. Happy to have escaped my close encounter that may have been my last call, I continued on my journey with a good and satisfied feeling.

PART 3
ONE MAN'S ESCAPE

Working as a brick shorter at the Djakarta harbor was actually not all that bad, taking into consideration that jobs for Dutch Indonesians were quite scarce. No one wanted to hire a half breed or Dutch citizen due to the political circumstances in Indonesia. Indonesian or Chinese companies would only hire Indonesian natives or Chinese workers. Consequently, on the broader side, it really paid off if someone was fortunate enough to have a friend in higher places. The Harbor Master of Tandjung Priok, the harbor of Djakarta, was a close friend of my father. He got me the job the same day I was desperately running away from my attackers. A Harbor Master's job was probably the most important job. He was in charge of the harbor – loading and un-loading of cargo, the incoming and outgoing vessel traffic, and money was made based on the total value of cargo in a year's time. Imported or exported goods were measured per square foot and in metric tons. Each ship was evaluated by weight and size. Most ships that came into the harbor were from international shipping lines. It was neat to see the different flags and nationalities parked beside each other in one place.

My father's friend wanted me to come and live with him and his family. In so doing, living in a very large home with comfort and servants, was a total change for me. Regardless of my situation or the circumstances I dealt with, the city of Djakarta was still a giant of a place even comparing it with New York, Tokyo or London. After a time it became somewhat uncomfortable for me since everything was provided to me by gardeners or house mates. Breakfast, lunch, dinner or anything else was served on a silver platter, served by hired na-tives. A Harbor Master made a huge salary, even then, and lived an outstanding life. For instance, he would spend most of his evenings playing bridge with other heads of corporations and was busy play-ing golf or racing cars on weekends.

Mr. van Dongen, the Harbor Master, was a white Dutch man and his family was from Holland. His wife and children were in my thoughts – sweethearts and the most beautiful people. It was some-thing someone could never forget, especially in my situation, being in a growing up stage and not having a family. Life under the most diffi-cult political circumstances was still good in the European community and it was still good under a Dutch social environment. Several of the well-suited European corporate heads were always giving money to Indonesian Generals or government officials under the table only to secure the lives of their families.

Despite the chances in better living conditions, it was still not what I wanted. I needed to leave Indonesia, the country of my birth for a better future. I had to finish my education in Holland. No one knows what lies in store for them. The white Dutch were hated by the Indonesian natives and for us, the Dutch Indonesians, we were half everything. The living conditions under President Soekarno became drastic and weary. The President ran an unstable and corrupt government causing the political parties to split. It gave an opportunity for the Communists to try to take over the country.

I sat down many evenings with the van Dongen family. Socializing as a family was really grand. It was like being at home with my own family. We had long talks together. Mr. van Dongen was a very understanding man and wrote my mother a letter about my attempt to leave the country. When the Roma came in to pick up hundreds of passengers, Mr. van Dongen visited the Italian Captain and made arrangements for me. I had to come aboard as a stowaway first. I was amazed that there were five other Dutch Indonesians were also aboard. One was a brick shorter like me and the others worked on the dock. The Italian crew was very helpful and slipped us through together with the other passengers. Our intent to escape the country now rested on the laps of Mother faith. In our minds, there was always a chance of being caught by the Indonesian harbor authorities and their military police units who searched the ships for stowaways.

The Captain and Purser took very good care of us and gave us uniforms and other necessities like soap, toothpaste, aspirin, underwear and towels. First, the crew found places for us to hide and they were good at it. While each of us was in our own hiding place, or as we called it our copy hole, the crew members graciously looked after us by supplying us with nourishment and soft drinks. We all liked the friendly smiles and the way the crew members made us feel. While The Roma took care of us aboard the ship, we were still waiting for goods to fill the cargo compartments. This made us, as stowaways, feel uneasy with the situation. It was strange how, under those circumstances, one could easily think up a storm and imagine wonderful things. I thought of New York City in America and lived for a moment in time in a fantasy world. I imagined sitting in a restaurant in Manhattan, enjoying good American food and watching people happily passing by. I thought of a delicious Coney Island hotdog or perhaps a cupcake and anything else that came to mind, what so many people take for granted. None of my friends nor I had ever been to Europe and this would be our first time. No matter what I knew that someday I would be in New York and I would be living in the land of unmatchable opportunities.

For her time in the 1950s, The Roma was, by far, a great luxurious liner and I was amazed by how ingenious the Italian ship builders could build with such style. From the dining room to each passenger cabin, all was designed for comfort and space. The whole interior of the ship had a flavor of elegance far beyond the years of her existence. This ship had transported more Dutch Indonesians over the seas and oceans than any other vessel at a time when Indonesia deported many of the Dutch Asiatic citizens and white Dutch out of the country.

After The Roma went out to sea and our ship was a half day out of Indonesian territorial waters, we had to see the Captain in his cabin. The Master of the Ship was heavy-set, but a friendly tough looking man and welcomed us aboard. He explained to us that we were hired on for the duration of the trip and we had to compensate for our trip by way of earning our fare. I thought it was fair not owing anyone anything and was ready to go to work. They placed one of my friends and me in the laundry room. How big the room was. I had to discover that even a simple laundry room aboard a passenger ship was full of energy and activity. My other friends received all different work details and every member of the crew treated us like their equals. That can't be said of other people that had different nationalities. Actually, it was fun working in the ship's laundry room with several other co-workers. My assignment was to fold clothes or hang suits.

When we left the cabin, the captain gave us each an envelope with Italian Lira and told us that he was glad to assist us to a brighter future. They found packing for us in temporary camps, outside the city of Naples, until the Dutch officials decided our future. The Italian government put up latrines, large sleeping tents and outside showers for us. This was an agreement the Dutch Royal House made with the city officials in Naples. All of us were so grateful for the warm Italian hospitality aboard the ship. Some of the officers and the Chief Engineer were willing to hire us. Obviously they liked our job performance. Folks in the laundry room called me "nit picky toothpick" for taking my job so seriously, which is my true nature. I always liked to earn my money through hard labor.

What was as interesting about The Roma as a ship was that she was a stream-lined luxurious passenger boat, and even by today's standards, the vessel was beautifully designed. She could crank up a top speed of 35 miles per hour in water. Everything that relates to cleanliness aboard was truly spotless – the floors, restrooms, kitchen, dining rooms, outside decks and doctor's offices. The money we earned aboard was used to buy goodies or other necessities. The bed I slept in was a hang-math and was just as comfortable as any other sleeping place.

For someone who had never seen the world, the sea trip was very interesting. Our first layover was in Singapore, a city all too familiar to me. When I was here in 1946, the city had so many Allied fighting men walking around. Even during the Western Colonial times, Singapore was considered the Pearl in the Malay Peninsula. Six years later I am back in the city for a visit. My friends and I decided to have a good night out and maybe meet some dates.

We went to "The Great World," a nightclub famous for dancing and drinking. The nightclub was mostly packed with sailors and officers. What made this peculiar place so interesting was how it was run. A sailor could buy a ticket for a dance and choose a girl to dance with him. The ticket was good for only one dance. The Eurasian girls were always attractive, full of adorable beauty and had the best of nature's gifts. Looking at their skin, one could only imagine looking at the wonderful pictures that move around. This is a major reason why many Allied men had gone ape in the place! Sailors of different nationalities were always getting along, until the most provoked situation arises. Then the inevitable fighting broke out as the women involved themselves with the men. During a fight, a uniform means nothing. Things had to be taken into consideration that men always fight other men. It was essential – man always needs to fight!

That particular evening, we were planning to have a good time. Some trouble began between British sailors and our Italian friends of The Roma. There were quite a few members of our ship in the nightclub. A couple of British seamen were jealous of the Italians and started to instigate trouble. Our friends of The Roma were having much better luck with the Eurasian girls than the Englishmen. Pretty soon the British sailors started to call the Italians "Magaroni's" because of their olive skin. They called us "Bloody Halfka's," which means half breeds. Before we could do anything, fights among the sailors broke out. As the very skinny youngster that I was, I had no intention of getting into a fight with anyone regardless of the circumstances. However, I got involved during the conflict.

A young Brit came charging at me and swung his broken beer bottle at my face. I immediately dove to the ground and with a fast body maneuver from the ground, I kicked the Brit with all my might in the groin. When the young man who attacked me fell to the floor, one of the huge Italian sailors who always fed me lifted me up and took me outside the club. As a big brother, he brought me back aboard. Whatever else happened that evening I would not find out until the next day.

After The Roma left Singapore, the luxurious liner steamed through the Indian Ocean and went on her way. Out at sea I could smell the air that was so different here. For the first time in my life I was able to observe a variety of color in the ocean's water and also saw that the color black was actually dark blue. One of nature's identities is that the black waters had steep and deep bottoms. Even modern submarines could not reach the depths below.

As nicely as our ship was cruising through most peaceful water, two days later we sailed toward the Red Sea and could feel unbearable heat. The heat that was felt aboard ship was absolutely draining and close to getting us exhausted. Many passengers were around the pool. Most crew members were not allowed to come near any of the passengers who were on deck: only Deck Stewards who served beverages. Many young women and teenage females were the cause of most of the attraction among the working men. At sea, it is very difficult to hold back on someone's passion for love, especially when a Seaman has been away from home for months. Two of the swimming pools aboard our ship were filled with bathing beauties and men showing off their Tarzan–like physiques. The men got nowhere with the beauties they were trying to impress. It was also fun to watch the children taking dives in the kid's section of the pool.

Interestingly to us was the first hand experience of watching our ship enter the Suez Canal after hearing many stories about the Canal and its history. How many lives had been involved in the project. When the Egyptian General Nazir came into power in 1956, he tore down the statue of the architect builder who built this unique artificial waterway for ships to pass through. For hundreds of years the French and English were domineering military forces in the Middle East. The decades of their presence were a major cause for Arab nations to rebel against Great Britain and France.

Slowly The Roma sailed through the Suez Canal and steamed into the Mediterranean Sea on course to Naples. We passed Malta by Gibraltar. Looking at the passage of time through history were all the events revolving between the Dutch, English, Portuguese and Spanish. How Germany and Great Britain fought each other in uncountable sea and air battles for total control. Gibraltar was a strategic fortress held by Allied military forces, in order for the Allies to maintain a stronghold overseeing the Middle East and Mediterranean.

Finally the moment came and The Roma was docked in Naples. The passengers were debarking and going off the ship to their own destinations. There were many passengers that came from Australia, India and other countries. The Dutch Indonesians or Dutch passengers had to wait their turn for their Italian guides who took them to the train station in Naples for Holland. We could not have any contact with them while aboard for political reasons since several of the Dutch Indonesians were our friends. In the meantime, the ship was getting empty from all the passengers leaving and the crew heading for home. We stood behind and waited for the officials to pick us up for our receiving camp. One thing about Italians, they could not hold time well. Mostly known to them was keeping break or lunch time on an appropriately slow pace. When they came to take us to our informal shelters, there were only six men on duty – a couple to guard the ship, one officer in charge of unloading procedures and the rest checking out The Roma.

After several hours of waiting, we were all very hungry. First they brought us to the Immigration Center for questions and answers. The officials here actually already had the information they needed for us to enter the country. When we left the harbor, the five of us who had stowed away were put in a bus and driven to our temporary camp. It was a hilly and rocky place outside the city overlooking Naples and was overrun with lava rock. The sleeping quarters as our contemporaneous residence was actually beautifully located. We had the most gorgeous view of the historical city. Three other guys and I shared a tent as roommates. We slept on WWI military field beds. In the middle of the tent was a small pot belly stove for us to burn wood in on cold nights. The ground we lived on was very dry and had many boulders and rocks. Quite a few other Dutch Indonesians that came before us had already lived in the same camp for quite a while. They placed several open showers near our tent; a few outhouses or latrines more toward the hillside and an open eating place. There was also a provision room were we could purchase our necessities and exchange towels. Two Italian cooks provided us our breakfasts and lunches. Living at the camp was not at all bad, except it was in the open sky, and we had nothing but the clothes that had been given to us by the crew of The Roma.

My tent mates and I had undertaken many trips to the city and enjoyed ourselves. We met new friends and some Italian families took us in as family members. They were so friendly and quite hospitable and always made us feel at home as soon as we arrived at their hous-es. Since our first meeting, I understood that Italian families enjoyed large parties for socializing and there was plenty of excellent food and wine. I loved the Italian culture. I took many trips to the art museums in Naples and, via a bus ride, also visited the ones in Rome. Always being astonished at the ingenuity of the Masters of the 14th and 15th centuries, I am sure innumerable artists from other parts of the world were influenced by them. These old Italian masters had many things in common with the Dutch masters of the same era.

The most incredible thing about Italian culture was that even the best of friends were always so loud when they engaged themselves in conversation. As an outsider one would think that these people were arguing. This was how Italians behaved in a friendly atmosphere.

Human nature, at times, could be given an outmost consideration that it was an illusion in which some people had dwelled through their own imaginative thinking. In their own failures they seemed to think that they perceive things the right way and take out their frustrations on weaker individuals. Some of those observations refer to some individuals who I considered the complainers in the camp. One of them was a young Dutch Indonesian who sometimes became outraged for no reason at all! This particular young man could not have been older than his early twenties and was trying to collect peti-tions from other people who lived in the camp. His biggest complaint was that the food was not good and the camp was badly managed. In all fairness to the Italians who were managing and the chefs who had been cooking for us did an outstanding job. We were all well fed and we always had clean clothes. The young spoiled ones just loved to pick on weaker and smaller individuals and intimidated others who did not like to fight back. My anger deep inside of me started to grow larger, and in order to prevent a confrontation with him, I decided to avoid coming near or even close to him. One thing my martial arts training always taught me was the art of surprise to eliminate physical oppression. Every fighting art was meant strictly for self defense. The young, arrogant Indo always had a very bad habit, which was to elbow passerbies with his left or right arm. When any of his elbows made a connection and someone started to tumble from the pain, he would enjoy the feeling of triumph from his physical contact and later brag about his hidden conquest. Aggravated as I often had become with him, this time around my chance came. I walked toward him, and when he started to notice me, I leaped into the air with a fast move, and laid a devastating knuckle sandwich between his eyes. He was in pain as I realized with delight that I had broken his nose. That ended his bizarre attitude toward others in camp and there were no more complaints.

A week after my confrontation with the Dutch Indonesian my uncle, who headed a small delegation of the Dutch Social Services, came to us and had a discussion with every individual who lived in the camp. Each of us was released from our camp and received new clothes and a heavy winter jacket for the winter in Western Europe. Finally, after all the escapades we were able to survive, we were allowed to go home to our Motherland. We thanked the Italian Camp Manager and cooks for the magnificent work they did for us. We left for the train station to travel to Holland.

PART 4
GOING BACK IN TIME TO KUN TAO

The old hand fist style of Chinese Kun Tao is more appropriately described as a humanistic methodology to the term for old fashion boxing that dates back to the beginning of man. The origin of modern man began in 16,000 BC when homo sapiens developed new and creative ways of inventing, exploring and culture building.

Modern man began to control the world and fought nature, wild animals and his own kind. Man started out first as a cave dweller, then became more advanced and discovered how to use fire to cook, forge tools and make weapons. Later on, man became ingenious by making surgical instruments through research and practice through thousands of years. The blacksmith who forged weapons and tools was also the first physician by discovering the art of healing during the cultural changes of older civilizations before ours.

In past and present, mortal combat was always in the nature of man to fight and survive. From the very beginning, homo sapiens fought each other; first on an individual level of man against man. As time evolved and cultures changed, man began a domineering factor where one man controls another. Greedy for more possessions, tribes started to migrate from one land to another, exterminating the first settlers when they found a weak society and established themselves as the habitants of a new land. They turned themselves from new settlers to land owners to nobility. The strongest always survived all living pressures prone to mankind. Throughout the centuries, settlers who inhabited their newly found countries became citizens of that country as historical recordings show. An example is found in the United States where the European settlers took away land from the American Indians.

Long before Christ, homo sapiens began to explore lands and nature, then dominated any humanistic obstacle that stood in their way. Individualistic combat was soon turned into an organized strategy for conquering others and their lands for economic gain. There were a great number of strategic geniuses who lived in the past. Alexander the Great is undisputedly considered as one of the world's greatest conquerors and was greatly skilled in military strategy, field coordination, languages and managing other countries he had occupied with his armies.

Afterward, other men followed in Alexander's footsteps through study of military conquests of the past and made themselves into emperors and rulers. The greatest strategists in military world history relate back to the endeavors of Hannibal, Genghis Khan and Napoleon. These men conquered more nations and lands and fought more battles than others. Their failure was their lust for greedy expansion and conquering others.

Being a native of Dutch descent, I have a curiosity about European and world history. The subjects were of great interest for understanding myself and my own martial arts studies. There is also cause for studying philosophy which leads to an understanding of one's own behavior in training for combat. My own nature is learning from the past. To understand one's own nature is practical. But better yet is to comprehend the nature of one's own self in becoming better through practice.

There are many reasons why I have made an extensive study of man's history and, in particular, the ventures of man in mortal combat. It has made me resourceful when dealing with others. In the very essence of my soul, I have lived in a spiritual sense, and without a doubt through the phase of historical events, and had to discover the values of war, strategy of mortal combat in an economy of motions. In order to enhance the art of combat, one needs to fully understand the nature of the beast in primitivism in man's culture and how it resides in each of us as individuals. I found it quite interesting, as a subject of psychological thinking, that tranquility and aggression are two of the same essences in complementing the roots of mortal combat.

Through a thought process in philosophy, the art of reasoning became greatly valued in our modern society as a social standard. It also based its essence on an art of law in psychological advances to higher learning in due process. The art of reasoning also relates to physical combat and strategic thinking.

Martial arts are generally understood as it relates to the Asian fighting arts, either unarmed or with armed weaponry. The Europeans may have left their influences behind in the diversified cultural exchanges between the Europeans and Eastern customs and traditions. The Europeans had the indigenous combat systems of boxing, wrestling and fencing. Alexander the Great introduced India to the arts of archery which was long before the Southeast Asians ever thought of using the bow and arrow for hunting and war. The spear was also a weapon introduced in Africa and India through the adventuresome expansion of Alexander when his army conquered the shores of India. Disease, illness and ill–fated planning to advance further into India bulked down Alexander's further advances. After seeking the advice of his generals, the Great Conqueror gave up his expedition and retreated to Europe.

Medieval combat started to develop in the nations inhabiting Europe and the Mediterranean. Russia and Germany were always at war. The Russians adopted the saying, "Who comes here with the sword will perish with the sword," during their defense of St. Petersburg in the 14th century battle with Germany.

While the rest of the world used unorganized methodologies for close quarters combat, China, in a sense, had created organized fighting arts for her armies. Many of the generals invented tactics in weaponry in the 4th Century BC. Chinese monks offered shelter and housing to the underprivileged. In the temple boxing schools, future monks were trained in the arts of war and also received an education to become scholars.

Before a monk was trained physically, he had to be taught the art of internal healing through self discipline and concentration. Focus was on breathing exercises. Medicine was formulated after careful studies and mixed with all sorts of herbs to make remedies to control diseases, longevity and better health.

Based on different philosophies, the temple boxing schools were divided religiously into Buddhism, Confuciousism, or Taoism. Through severe self discipline in meditation, diet and training, the monks applied their mental skills to their martial arts.

Relating to combative systems, the temple boxing schools became separated between the Northern styles and Southern styles. In North China, Kung Fu was primarily practiced by the larger Chinese of Mongolian descent. The individuals who practice Northern styles like to refer to their combative arts as "high mountain ranges," because of their huge structure in physicality. They use long and high extended forceful kicking techniques. Their brutal hitting is always highly noticeable for their use of long, extended kicks.

Chinese Kun Tao is a term used by the most common man that came from South China and settled in Indonesia some 4000 years ago. Many mass migrations throughout the vast length of Southeast Asia had taken place. Several hundred nomads from Tibet and China came to live there in the newly found land in many of the islands in the East Indian archipelago. Those migrating tribes of people (mostly Hakka nomads) succeeded at becoming very prosperous in their new environment after centuries of hard labor. They created their own businesses and established much wealth from their means of making a living. Each Chinese merchant or contract laborer had to protect his family and goods from natives and even his own kind. Many of the merchants had trained in China in various arts of self defense to protect themselves from being harmed.

The Chinese were considered foreign intruders by the native Indonesians. The Chinese created then secret Chinese Shao Lin Societies and established underground martial arts schools which only permitted Chinese students. In the city of Palembang there were, at one time, seven (7) groups of Shao Lin temple boxing schools. Years later (up to the 1930's), the schools disappeared and were never seen again. Several of the teachers who taught in any of those schools went wide spread over the length of the Indonesian Archipelago and had gone with their own. These Kun Tao Masters were settling in cities like Djakarta, Bogor, Bandung, Semarang, Surabaya, and Maccasar in Celebes.

A reason why practitioners of Chinese Kun Tao had always kept to themselves, but were highly noticed even among the best Silat practitioners and in the circles of European communities, was because of their deadly combat skills. The training in Kun Tao is second to none in physical practice, endurance, the study of the internal and healing arts and the art of self discipline. Every form of Kun Tao comprises those elements in a method of training. A Kun Tao expert can be considered a "whole" man once he has grown through the mature studies. Studies in the Chinese fighting arts also include understanding animals as they behave in relation to man, and comprehension of one's self in relation to nature.

While in South China, practitioners of the South adopt themselves rather close to the fighting arts and lower kicking techniques for short distances. Both systems of temple schools in the North and South had, over the centuries, discovered new methods of mortal combat through hard labor. 3600 fighting styles of organized combat developed out of the various Shao Lin schools.

The word "Kung Fu" relates only to refined skills and may not always be meaningfully expressed as a combative gesture in North

China. Depending how the word is actually used in a table conversation, someone from South China may understand the refined skills as Gung Fu. There are many ways the combative arts can be expressed in language and all relate to Wu Shu or the Military Arts of War.

Before the development of Chinese boxing arts took place, temple boxing schools highly influenced the martial arts practices from Mongolia to Manchuria. The refined combative arts from the Mongols brought in as a contributing factor to the Shao Lin arts: combative systems of grappling, throwing, striking, punching, kicking and the art of bone breaking. After centuries of intense training, the Chinese fighting arts were noted by the rest of the world as the falling, rolling, striking and throwing arts the Chinese referred to as Ju Jitsu or the art of Chi Chuan.

At one time, Jigoro Kano, the founding father of Japanese Judo in the 1930s, made his art and art of studies to perfection. Japanese Judo that came first from Chinese Judo was later highly respected and practiced all over the world. Kano died in 1938 and was unable to enjoy the fruits of his labors. The founder of Japanese Aikido, O' Sensei Uchiba, after encountering a Chinese Baqua expert in Hong Kong, lost in combat and later created his beautiful art of Aikido. Considered as the refined art of soft skills, Judo and Aikido were the most considered martial arts of the 19th and 20th centuries.

PART 5
PROSPECTIVES OF A PHILOSOPHICAL POINT OF VIEW

It is hard to explain how self discipline is sometimes the best experience. One is able to enhance him or herself by just placing a mindset, for whatever it's worth, in a tranquil environment. Undisturbed, the mind can reach a distance of unlimited range. From my experience, self discipline pertains to absolute calmness; to understand the intent of anguish and how to grasp or reach out to the mindset of others. Perfection is something that is never a factor in the existence of life. Only by assuming things can be "perfect" is to distinguish and satisfy our own needs.

Imagination enables a mental excursion, the ability to travel somewhere else on this planet and discover new things. The downside of any imaginary frontier is when someone dwells in a fantasy world. At times it is good to live in a fantasy world and other times it leads to inventing reality in a fictitious world.

In a prosperous thought process, one can always reach a moment in time that only valued things can be an acceptable means in the human gesture. Only in humbling oneself to the true nature within can the purity of truth be observed in being alive.

Considering that I have gone through the pages of historical events, I would like to share some topics after reading about the wisdom of some highly noted scholars from China. One of the most famous scholars and educators was to my liking. It was the warrior and scholar Chuang Tzu, the teacher of Lao Tzu. "There is nothing in the world greater than a bird's feather. None have lived longer that a dead child and old Peng Tzu died young. Heaven and Earth grow together with me and a thousand things and I are one. Yet I have just said we are one, so my words exist also. Even a skilled mathematician cannot reach the end, much less an ordinary man. If we proceed from nothing to something to something, [is it] enough? Let us stop."

Taoism is not a religion but a philosophical thought in the progression of understanding life. It is living a philosophy. What makes a Taoist is that they are survivors of the extreme. Of my own practice of Kun Tao, I also understand that I had to accept things for what they are worth and also to accept things that I could not reach. What more is there to reach? Only the things that can be seen can be reached.

Chuang Tzu was the father of Taoism. Lao Tzu had set forth

Chuang Tzu's wisdom in a philosophical thought process and made the thought of wisdom a deep learning process. Confucianism was during a time when Lao Tzu brought spiritual freedom to the masses who became his followers.

Through the practice of training in Chinese Kun Tao, I had sincere focus of understanding in what I was doing. Chinese Kun Tao as a means of self defense also helped me to find peace, tranquility and harmony of the soul. It gave me the inheritance of a most serene quietude and a restful heart. When training, I am the most aggressive man. After my training, I am the most peaceful man. As a teacher and martial arts leader, I have taught many men, women and children of diverse backgrounds in the martial arts. My accomplishments were many and of a pleasant nature to most people, but not all. We are all human beings. That would mean nothing if not for my wife. She always stood beside me, from dawn to dawn and from horizon to horizon. The greatest part of my life that made me a successful man has always been my wife, Joyce Helen de Thouars. She has helped me in experiencing a rightful life.

The three "father-teachers" (rightfully sigungs) who taught the family art of Wu Kung and Hak Ka were the three Honorable Masters: Sigung Tan Tong Liong (old Shao Lin), Sigung buk Chin (Internal Arts) and Sigung Willem Chang (External Arts). These men were always the greatest inspiration to me and their guidance has never left my soul. They taught me their family art of Wu Kung Kun Tao. Wu meaningfully expressed as actions of war. It relates to the practice of the movements of the tiger, the leopard, the monkey, the twin dragon and the eagle (mentis).

By explaining the physical expression of bodily movements in practice, the lion distinguishes itself as a great compliment to the dragon. During ceremonies and festivities, the lion is role-played with a lion dance with two players. One is the tail and the other functions as the head. While the dragon dance is the total opposite of the lion dance performance. With the dragon, 12 to up to 18 players are performing the celebration dance. The music of the gongs is basically the same rhythm. When the gongs have a faster beat the players follow accordingly. When the beat is slower, the movements are tempered down.

Long ago merchants would place money in a rice paper basket and put it on top of a high pole for tranquility and good luck. The envelopes were tight with strings way up high and the lion dancers, in particular, had to stand on the top of each other's shoulders to reach the top of the pole. When there were two lion dance groups involved, fights would sometimes break out during a dance performance as each group tried to reach the top at the same time. They would push each other aside and the falling party would usually start a fight action. It is very interesting to watch, especially when Northern and Southern styles are used. Actions in the street with the participants fighting made the day for those watching the event.

The tree sigungs were the disciples of the Grandmaster of the system. He was Tao Sigung or Dar Mor-Liem Ping Wan. Only sigungs under him, like my three father teachers always function in harmony as three brother teachers and each master has a specialty. It was learning the system from three perspectives. From Liem Ping Wan to the three sigungs, alcohol was used and most of the time they were healthy drunk. Their alcohol intake was beyond anyone's imagination, and it slowed them down to an extent. But they were the best at how Kung Fu could really be expressed, in the caring of "true" experts that had deep comprehensive knowledge of what they were practicing.

When I left Indonesia with only the clothing I wore, I lost many invaluable pictures of my past. I will honor my teachers starting with the grandfather teacher, Liem Ping Wan and then onto the other teachers. I have illustrated them with my drawings. I hope they approve of my intent. All four of them, the most gracious and honorable Kun Tao coaches, have folded their hands and left me alone with a job to do. I promised them my lifetime commitment to teach their art. Hopefully I have done a good job for them.

My most honorable and gracious teachers always followed the nature of the drunk but wise scholar, the poet Li Po Chang, for whom I adopted his philosophy of understanding life at age 67. In trying to follow in my teachers' footsteps, it is also my belief to reach out in spirit and to live as a small shadow in the footsteps they left me to follow.

An illustration of grandmaster–teacher or Tao Sr Sigung Lama Darmor or Liem Ping Wan (1875–1942) in his late 60's.

In each of the father teachings, the sigungs had a specialty of his own. They taught their family system of Wu Kung and Hak Ka Kun Tao to just a few hand-picked students that later became their disciples. Tan Tong Liong, for instance, taught his specialty of Tibetan Shao Lin and called his way of practice "The Peaceful Forest" style. It was a South Central Chinese form of combat, but also a specific family style. It came through the teachings of the honorable Tao Sr Sigung Liem Ping Wan.

Training the art under Sigung Liem was "fatherly" like with many hardships in training. The duration of each training session was brutal and painstaking. He taught seven Kun Tao forms: pai ching, pai hung, wu kung, chuan shu and tung lung tai. They all had to be done very low, structured with lots of duck walking for 700 yards up and down hill. On each shoulder hangs a bag loaded with rocks. And each duck walk training session took students through hours of low training, at times with everyone near collapse. We called this the ma du low horse training and it was a first basic event.

Coming back the next day, we continued training by standing in a very low horse stance for an hour at a time. In order to measure a correct low horse stance, we had to put a stick on our upper leg structure. When the stick did not slide off our horse stance, the low horse position was okay. If it did roll off, we had to compromise and lower our horse stance position. This was the training schedule for the next six months when a student was accepted by a teacher. Part of the training included doing home work like scrubbing floors and cooking meals for the teacher.

Training under Sigung Liong followed for another six months. We trained in a standing still horse stance and meditated into seeing nothing, hearing nothing and began work on soft breathing exercises. Later soft breathing was combined with more forceful exhalation to combat bad breath control.

After a year of training almost four days per week, students were checked out. Almost no one failed, because the students were aware of the necessity in learning Kun Tao. They say that Kung Fu represents a rock that cannot be moved and is placidly positioned. What this relates to is the art of rooting. A reason why the duck walking and standing still horse stances training happens in low positions is so it teaches the lower stomach muscles to work harder.

The following year, we had gone through the Pung, Cha and "T" training out of the same low horse stance that we learned in our first Kun Tao practice. Pung was explained to me as a motion to block in various ways. Cha explains itself as an artful description of a variety of methods for kicking and striking. "T" signifies itself as the different kicks, leg traps, and sweeps and take downs with the lower body.

Father Teacher Liong was a very short tempered Sigung. Training in his sessions was mostly done in his kwoon, a small room in his establishment, or totally outside in the forest. It was the best time I ever had in my experience of martial arts training. We trained for hours and became either boring or interesting. Repetition was a major cause of boredom among my fellow training mates. They were all like extended family. I described in my first autobiography some of the situations for being accepted as a non-Chinese in a traditional Kun Tao school. This is my follow up as my second book.

After two years of practice and learning the "same old thing" over and over again – simplified in low horse stances, blocking, kicking, throwing each other to the ground and pulling elephant grass with two fingers (or twin dragon) – we overcame the painstaking events in our battered legs. In fact, every inch of our nervous system became so well accustomed to our training that our training became the seed the father teacher planted in our souls.

Finally, they the third year, Sigung Liong began to train us in forms. That was a real torture and he used a measurement tool just to check how low we had gotten in our horse stances. We were allowed to come with both our buttocks only ten inches or less above the ground. The forms had to be fully expressed with energy. One has to give it all he was able to give. As a reward for him teaching us, he demanded more energy and for us to go even lower. This is the reason why Kun Tao training is severe and harsh training and done in a traditional Kun Tao school. I have never seen a sloppy Kun Tao form. It is always done fast and full of energy and stamina.

Below is an illustration of Sigung Tan Tong Liong (1890–1959) teaching the Pai Ching form. It was customary in the olden days that Kun Tao Masters wore shorts in combat. Short pants are harder to grab than long pants.

The philosophy as a source for our tranquil progression through the Kun Tao system, as taught by Taoist teachers, came through the poetry of a drunk, wandering poet. The poet Li Po Chang and his poetry have inspired me since my introduction to Kun Tao. Li Po Chang wrote many masterpieces that were well received in Japan and Korea. He was totally superb in his thinking and wrote best when he either had a hangover or was intoxicated with wine. Drunks and children are the most truthful and Li Po saw the wonders and glory of the world when he was happily drunk on his wine. While drunk during his retreat in the mountains and while watching the water flowing in the Chang Tze River, he was at his best. Here is one of the Master's poems.

THE UNSPOKEN WORDS

WHENCE THESE TWELVE PEAKS OF Wu-Shan!
Have flown into gorgeous screen.
From heaven's one corner?
Ah, those lonely pines murmuring in the wind!
Those palaces of Yang–Tai, hovering over there –
Oh, the melancholy of it! –
Where the jeweled cough of the king
With brocade cover desolate, –
His elfin maid voluptuously fair
Still haunting them in vain!

Here a few feet
Seem a thousand miles.
The craggy walls glisten blue and red.
A piece of dazzling embroidery.
How green those distant trees.
Round the river strait of Ching-Men!
And those chips – they go on.
Floating on the waters of Pa.
Between countless hills.
Of shining mist and lustrous grass.

How many years since these valley flowers bloomed
To smile in the sun?
And that man traveling on the river,
Does he not for ages hear the monkeys screaming?
Whoever looks on this,
Loses himself in eternity;
And entering the scared mountain of Sung,
He will dream among the resplendent clouds.

LI PO CHANG, the Wandering Poet
(701–762 CE)

Under Sigung Buk Chin there was a totally different physical and internal education for endurance and also a comprehensive understanding of the internal analytics in observation. Most was based upon the principles and physics in the workings of the breathing system. Through Gi Gung or Chi Kung exercises, practice pertains to a total commitment to health. The opposite of health practice is another breathing exercise – the practice of Nei Gung stomach exercise training. Its purpose is to aid in the rejection of outside forces to penetrate the body internally. Nei Gung is an internal, defensive art that takes in severe blows, kicks and forceful palm strikes. It is mainly practiced by the practitioner in Nei Gung to protect the body from being harmed. The Wei Kung art training is a form of aggressively breathing with the purpose of countering external or internal attacks. Most of the exercises in this breathing art are very energetic and explosive with the intent of penetrating the nerves, internal and circulatory systems of the opponent. In some instances, death may occur with a delayed reaction in the bloodstream. A trained practitioner can easily penetrate the nerve center, the muscle and bloodstream of an opponent with a soft finger touch or a light palm strike targeted at specific anatomical regions of the body. When the three internal principles were studied intensively in training, any practitioner with years of experience will use Gi Gung, Nei Gung and Wei Kung as one art in action.

Forms are important to practice for the understanding a purpose of learning forms. It is also a greater health remedy in practice because every limb, muscle and tissue, whether internal or external, are continuously moving. Forms are purposely designed to serve their purpose for the comprehension of seeing oneself in harmony with the feeling of the movements. A form is, realistically speaking, an art of moving with technical values and for the understanding of the fighting art. Chinese martial arts strongly emphasize that a student know his art. The better you know your art, the better you will know yourself. What you do with any form will help you form a better understanding of yourself.

Sigung Buk Chin was the internal master from the three father teachers and spent a lifetime of internal training in the forest of China. He trained in Tai Chi Chuan, I Shing Yie and Pa Kua – the only three internal styles in the classics of Chinese Temple boxing. The most known of the combative arts was practiced mostly in the Wu Tang temple boxing school. Wu Tang was named after the movements of the wild boar, which attack with fierce aggression. Obviously, after years of practice, the fighting monks of Wu Tang had adopted and brought the aggressive movements of the wild boar into the Wu Tang fighting arts.

The three internal arts – Tai Chi Chuan, Pa Kua and I Shing Yie – were predominantly practiced in the Wu Tang temple boxing school. Besides having influenced the other styles of Shao Lin boxing arts, the Wu Tang remained the heart of the temple boxing school in China. All the major fighting styles out of Wu Tang found their influences through the wild boar aggressive movements. Fighting styles like the Fut Ga, Hungga, Mai Hung, Tan Tu'I, Low Han and Choy Li Fat came out of the Wu Tang temple boxing school. The most noticed and respected Shao Lin art of Wu Tang was Fut Ga and is known historically as the art of assassins.

Intense practitioners in the Fut Ga system were also considered the protectors and guardians of the Wu Tang temple. Through all of Shao Lin's history, emperors or rich land owners hired Fut Ga boxers to assassinate anyone who was a threat to the ruling nobility. Fut Ga as a fighting art comprises a lot of Tai Chi Chuan, I Shing Yie and Pa Kua in the combative side of the art.

A well trained master of the art, Sun Kung sifu Dai Yung (1895– 1937) introduced this Chinese boxing art in Hawaii during the 1930's. His successor, Sigung Arthur Lee, is still teaching Fut Ga in Hawaii. The Sil Lum Fut Ga Institute is located in Honolulu. Since the art is a "rare" system of Shao Lin, I would recommend anyone who is interested in the art to look Sigung Lee up. The address of the school in Honolulu is:

1024 Smith Street
Honolulu, HI 96817
Phone/Fax: 808–599–4690

Father teacher Buk Chin was Wu Tang trained. His main objective for training his hand picked disciples was to teach them the internal art. He named a form specifically to honor the drunk, wandering poet Li Po Chang and to respect his teacher, Liem Ping Wan. He taught just a few individuals, including myself, the three internal forms: I Shing Po, Wa Kwa and Tai Keh.

An illustration of Father Teacher Sigung Buk Chin (1895–1960) in a very low fighting horse stance, the Ma Bu Chuen.

It was through the system of Chinese Kun Tao that I was able to improve through the severity of training considered to be an internal-external system. The forms that I had to study were mostly external old Shao Lin forms. Out of the 50 forms, only five are able to be distinguished as internal practice. Tai Keh, I Shing Yie and Pa Kua are the main ingredients and backbone to strengthen the energy behind the movements. The fighting capability for a practitioner of the system are strengthen when the three principles are combined to form one fighting principle.

Lastly the father teacher Sigung Willem Chang was responsible for teaching Northern Shao Lin to our small group of disciples in the combative arts. The three master teachers were totally different from one another and in their styles of teaching. Their amazing skills were also opposite. Highly noticed as skillful masters in Kun Tao, the three masters were quite unique in approaching martial arts and in relating to people. When they fought outsiders, one did not need to be an expert in any form of combative art to notice that the men they were watching were nothing more than walking and mauling human fighting machines with skills and enduring energy. What the masters were practicing was the "old hand" Kung Fu. All the money or treasures of the earth cannot replace the presence of these honorable teachers in the serenity of my soul.

The way the three men were observed by people in the street or by merchants in open markets or by other fighting arts experts was mostly by their presence and look. Awesome for their physical presence, it was scary to see them walking around. People immediately noticed that these men were ready to go to combat with anyone that felt like taking them on. It did not matter if they were alone or together as three warriors, their presence alone demanded instant respect.

Looking at my teachers so many years ago, I had a sense of pride and always wanted to be like them. I wanted all three in my soul and I knew that those me who taught me left something in me. How privileged I felt then, 63 years ago, and still feel now. I knew it then that they were the true warriors. They were always drunk and followed in the footsteps of the most drunken poet the world has ever known. Li Po Chung was our spiritual leader throughout our living and adventuresome martial art endeavors.

What was unique about my Kun Tao teachers was that by observing, for instance Tan Tong Liong, you could not help but notice that they were of slender build and equipped with long, lean muscle and overwhelmed with non-stop, tirelessly expressed energy. Looking at father teacher Buk Chin, this man was stocky, short and moved vastly around as second to none. He was here and there and always intimidating looking at other fighting experts. What was really amazing was that this little but well-equipped man with muscles could move around so fast that it looked like every step he made hardly touched the ground.

As a contrast to the two other teachers was Sigung Willem Chang who stood out huge in physical strength and was loaded with a well muscled and toned body. Surprisingly a large man like him was very light on his feet and very quick when he moved or when intercepting someone's automatic reaction. I would also like to add a descriptive illustration of Sigung Willem Chang in this part of my writing.

Willem Chang (1899–1959)

PART 6
THE OLD TIMES

It is never easy to recollect my time studying Kun Tao under a Chinese teacher. Even though I was selected as a student by my teacher, most of the other students who trained in the kwoon were all Chinese disciples. To them, I was a rude intruder, trying to steal the martial arts secrets that should be taught only to Orientals. I had a most unpleasant experience while under the same roof with my brothers in the Art. That was over 50 years ago, and lucky for the cultural exchanges, things have turned in favor of anyone who is really interested in training in martial arts.

Accepting my situation, I went on and became a great listener for instruction from the senior practitioner or my father teacher, Tan Tong Liong. He eased my mind after he told me in inhale the abusive treatment and to let nothing stand in my way. He was so right. Psychologically, it made me a better practitioner and philosophically it taught me to be a better thinker.

Taking any "sound" advice with deep consideration, I had become a lot stronger mentally and physically. I walked easily as a large man, but moved over the floor like a bird's feather. Nothing bothered me. It was a great learning tool for overcoming any mental obstacle.

Being a martial arts practitioner for many years, I would like to share some pencil illustrations, mainly of body positioning, and share the fighting art of Wu Kung Kun Tao with my friends. This will allow them to gain a "slight" understanding of the art I practice. As an artist I am able to sketch and draw figures. The most important part of Kun Tao training is the low or medium horse stance or the Ma Bu. A student of Kun Tao should be able to stay in one place and in a very low position for a prolonged period of time. Through intense self discipline, one should be able to overcome the painful stress in the knees and lower legs. While standing in a very low horse position, one should be in complete harmony with nature and himself. When the mind stands still, the body is still active and supple. When the mind is active, the body is resting in peace.

The following pages show several of my illustrations concerning the meditative position in calmness and how the spirit in practicing Kun Tao has to feel, in a sense, the spirit of animals. It is in our true nature! All drawings and materials in this book are copyrighted.

The following pages of drawings relate to the body positioning and movements of insects and animals. These are the dragon, tiger, leopard, praying mantis, eagle and monkey.

Dragon Tail Wu Kuen Kun Tao

The "ferocity" of the macaque monkey posture has always influenced most of the martial arts from Indonesia. The energy in the aggressive movements can hardly be described. It is relentless and full of energy.

The might of the eagle and eagle talon.

The most feared carnivorous predator in the insect world has to be the praying mantis. It dines on small field mice, small birds and anything else of flesh. Always standing relaxed, the praying mantis lashes out at its prey with lightening speed. Its front legs are designed to strike or grab.

I decided to write an extra page devoted to the black leopard. I treasure and honor this animal. This beast of magnificence has become rare to see even in the wild. They are still roaming in the densely populated areas in the forests of Southeast Asia, India and Africa. They are close to extinction due to poachers and trophy hunters. It is my intent, through the sale of my artwork, the support the different foundations that protect these treasured wild animals.

The wolverine, snow leopard and black leopard are large cats that are particularly in need of protection. I am a supporter of hunting for food and to help control some animal populations that may otherwise starve due to their numbers. My own personal war is with the trophy hunters and people who drink the blood of snakes and use tiger bones for medical remedies. The greed of humans is fed by the fixation of some that tiger bones will strengthen herbal remedy mixtures. Drinking cobra blood is insanity or killing monkeys to eat their brains is human insanity.

The reason I practice Kun Tao is that it's training in the spirit life of animals, which has been misunderstood in man's civilized world. In particular the strength, suppleness and agility of the black leopard, one of the most ferocious members of the cat family, comes unnoticed and unheard. It is a silent killer. There was a story recorded in a Dutch newspaper in the 1950s of a black leopard that jumped and killed a lion while the lion was trying to eat its dinner.

By choice I used the black leopard as an example in my drawing. This is not to take away from the spotted leopard or jaguar as these two cats are the most aggressive in the leopard family. When it comes to painting or drawing animals, they are by far my preference for leading players in my stories. People in the martial arts practice enjoy practicing to be an animal.

The journey of my martial arts career will end in December, 2010 and several of my senior disciples or longtime practitioners will continue to set forth the seeds I planted for them to progress the art further. My total devotion will be expressing my feelings on canvas or paper to the wild kingdom of mammals, insects, reptiles and birds of prey.

Always low to the ground or in a crouched position in a tree, the black leopard comes out of nowhere and is ready to jump or surprise its prey from humans or other predators. Humans are also considered predators of the "worst kind." They also stalk others to rob and kill. This page shows a black leopard ready to jump, a position used in our animal Kun Tao art.

The Java tigers became extinct in the early part of the 1950s. Considered to be the smallest of the tiger species, this cat grew to weigh between 200 and 250 pounds. The Java King tiger had a large head and was considered one of the most ferocious and aggressive large cats. When driven by hunger, it would attack a rhino or elephant. It is assumed that there may still be some tigers left in the dense areas of Java's forests where it is hidden from humans.

In concluding Chapter 6, I would like to express my feelings about the reptile world. Aside from my passion for martial arts, this is my second nature by birth, my admiration for the animal world – large cats, insects and crawling creatures, runs deep. I also admire birds of prey. The wild kingdom, generally speaking, has my devotion and true love. To draw with pencils and put these creatures on canvas is the way to show my feelings to the world. Animals need to be protected from the men with guns who kill for the sake of killing.

Considering that reptiles are also high on my priority list of species needing protection, my most favorite reptile is the rattle snake. Its instant actions of striking and biting at the same time are amazing. The most unique experience I had was with a mountain rattler. I once witnessed a rattle snake striking out of a bush at a rabbit. It killed it instantly. Actually, I still thank that rabbit for being in front of me and my students that day. We went out as a group outside the city of Boulder to do mountain training in the summer of 1988.

We looked down at the reptile and the dead rabbit. It immediately started to rattle as a warning for us to not come near him. To my astonishment, the snake was trying to swallow the rabbit whole just as a large python would eat his prey. Back in Java, a full grown python can grow to be thirty feet long and weigh 200 pounds. It takes five strong individuals to carry such a gigantic snake around.

While reptiles are the most misunderstood creatures on earth, they also serve a purpose as a species. The cobras in Asia, India and Africa minimize the population of rats. I include a list of snakes that are very poisonous. The most highly toxic snakes are cobras, branded krait, European adders, horned vipers, puff adders, and water moccasins, Eastern and Western rattlesnakes, coral snakes, Java warts and the aersculapilan snake. Treat snakes with respect and keep your distance. I am mentioning snakes from all over the world since most of us are world travelers. Every living species has the right to live for its existence.

My favorite will always be the rattlesnake for its speed. Cobras are quick when they strike or spit at their victim, but a mongoose has the ability to outmaneuver a cobra's attack and kill the reptile. When a rattlesnake is coiled in a spiral, it is quick and will strike with lightening speed at anything that moves. The mongoose would not have the chance to escape the rattler's focus of interest.

Despite my fascination with reptiles, the rattlesnake will always be my main focus when it comes to snakes. Rather than taking a cobra as my example for body positioning in practice of Kun Tao fighting in my training, my preference will remain the rattlesnake. Snakes are beautiful and dressed with the colors of the rainbow.

In the drawing underneath, a rattlesnake is uncoiling and lashing out to strike.

PART 7
HA KA KUN TAO IN INDONESIA

How can anyone really describe the history of the fighting art of Kun Tao? The best way to experience Kun Tao is by actually getting involved and training in a system of Kun Tao. There are many various ways in which Kun Tao as a boxing art has been practiced by many practitioners of the fist arts around the world.

From my perspective, I like to relate to any practice of fighting as a boxing art that combines hitting and grabbing into one was of using hands and legs. To me, it was explained by my teachers that Kun Tao, although it has a variety of diverse practices of combat, came out of the Hokien dialectic expression of the art of the fist in brutal fighting. The most common man used the word. In many instances, the people involved were street brawlers.

My involvement in the practice of the art relates back to my three teachers who taught me this Southern Chinese fighting art. My main reason for considering my teachers as father teachers were because they functioned as "guiding fathers" and were skilled to kill people if they wished. They had combat skills that were far beyond others I had seen at that time.

What was instantly instilled in me was that they always taught me to remain humble and to understand myself before even trying to comprehend the working of nature. My teacher belonged to a special group of "old" Kun Tao practitioners who called themselves the "old" Fu Jaws or Tiger Crane Fighters. They came from a generation of combat practitioners who had faced death many times in their past.

Interestingly for me as a fighting arts practitioner is that the Southern Chinese fist style my teachers taught me was highly influenced by the principles of Tai Chi Chuan, Pa Kua and I Shing Yie. Besides being fully trained in the external art, a chosen disciple in any Chinese fist art also must understand appropriate breathing techniques. These techniques can only be understood by enhancing the practice of using the nervous system as a defense system.

The old family style the three teachers were practicing was Kun Lun Pai. Kun Lun Pai is a fist-fighting art dating back to the 18th century. It is a Kun Lun mountain tradition of fighting and the source fits appropriately with the surroundings that draw its nature back to the steep and high mountain ranges between Tibet and South China.

Many Mongolian tribesmen settled with their families on the rugged and steep sides of the Kun Lun mountains, which prevented intruders from coming near them. They brought with them their own Ha Ka culture, customs and traditions along with a variety of colorful art work and written language. The three masters came to the Dutch East Indies in the 1920's. They were forced to leave China because they killed their landlords and unworthy tax collectors.

I was acquainted first with Liem Ping Wan, our Ha Tang Sifu who out of the kindness of his heart had compassion for me as a weak child. He worked with me to teach me breathing exercised to increase my stamina. I had never seen anyone that had gone beyond this "old" man's martial arts skills and was set apart from other skillful fighters. He had the most incredible expertise when it came to the internal fighting arts.

At the time of my experience with the little Chinese –Tibetan store owner, it was far above anything else I had ever seen before. He could kill if he wanted with just a slight twist of his finger by penetrating the internal system of his opponent. As I once saw, he easily side stepped a charge of a 1500 pound full grown water buffalo. With one strike of his palm, he brought the beast to his knees and killed him.

Liem Ping Wan was 67 when I knew him. He had an incredible capability to seize and even kill a large, wild water buffalo with no effort. He had to save me from being trampled by the charging animal at a market place. When they dissected the animal, they found a white palm imprint in the center of the bull's brain. It was obviously the side that the old man penetrated when he struck the center of the large head.

The ease with which the old store owner moved around made other fighting experts look like school children. Everyone that had known the old man in the 1930's and 1940's feared him not for his martial arts skills, but for his internal technical skills. He could unleash a soft vibrating touch with his fingers to any anatomical region of an individual and death would occur through a delayed movement in the nervous system.

The few individuals who were lucky enough to receive a little bit of training under the old Chinese store owner were also taught to use the "heavy hand" or vibrating palm. A vibrating palm technique is the opposite of Iron Palm hands breaking. Seasoned practitioners in the vibrating palm use their skills with exact timing in an attack to stop the regular blood flow on the beat of the heart. Through a penetrating touch through the muscles and veins, a cyclic change is created in the healthy blood stream. It will simply stop the flow of blood from reaching the heart. A palm expert uses excessive force to hit or strike.

The grandfather teacher, Liem Ping Wan, died in 1942 after a confrontation with the Japanese military police. His three disciples and most qualified practitioners in his system continued teaching his combative art family style. They taught only individuals worthy of their time. Chinese fighting arts experts became opposed to teaching non–Chinese students their secrets. Any form of communication with them ends with a silent treatment and only in business can there be an exchange for verbal communication to be established. They are close knit and shunned outsiders that came close to their facility or comfort zone.

In the tradition of Kun Tao, a chose student was always hand picked. Once he was taken in he became a member of the extended family and was taught philosophy, history, customs, healing arts, Chinese medicine and fighting arts. Additionally, hand picked students also performed housework, cooking and artwork as a form of meditation.

Patience as a virtue of hope was the first requirement a chosen student had to learn. The ability to understand the humbling and comprehension of mental endurance and seeing one's own mirror image of the warrior within was required.

The training in which each student had to go through was comprised mostly of the basic very low horse stance for hours at a time. There were variable basic training structures for the just the fundamentals of training in old hand Kung Fu. After many years of learning how large scale the fighting art of Kun Tao is, someone would need to be at least 200 years old before they completely scratched the surface of the variety of this fighting art.

The studies of Shao Lin relates in many instances to the disciplines that can be considered as a higher level of studies. The philosophy upon which I base my thinking on during the years of my training, and also later life, taught me more than just the ability to receive simple instructions from my Kun Tao masters.

When comparing an academic education to comprehensive Kun Tao studies, there is no linear comparison. Academic students learn language, modern technology and science. Then they find employment and continue to search for higher job placements. They also must experience the devastation of a sad economic world. After retirement, any diploma achieved at a college or university is only a wall decoration. With the physical and mental studies of old hand Kung Fu, there is no wall decoration. Only the fruits of one's laboring efforts for longevity in better health.

Most of the Kun Tao styles, Northern or Southern, have been greatly influenced by Southern Hung Ga Shao Lin. In previous times, the low horse stances were the core in practice as a way of life by the Hung Ga people who lived, worked, trained and conducted business all their lives on boats. They were known throughout the martial arts world as the boat people and their punishing fighting art of Hung Ga.

Wu Kung in the old hand Kung Fu has a lot of variation of combat and is referred to as Wu Kung. Explaining Wu can be easy in the Southern Chinese dialect as explosiveness in actions in a trained behavior. The example of Kung relates to all the fighting skills enhanced after years of training. The two elements of Wu and Kung combined in a fighting art pertains to the use of armed and unarmed combat. A Wu Kung attack by a skilled practitioner in this particular system of fighting is fully attacking with the aggression to penetrate an opponent's defenses with fast, unleashed, punishing strikes, eye poking and following up with devastating shin kicks. Everything is done with lightening speed and each attack is purposely designed to destroy and enemy's anatomical region.

The very low postures were influenced by the Wu Tang Temple boxing school as were the leg maneuvering skills and lightening speed movements. The Wu Kung practitioners were always highly respected everywhere for their fighting capabilities and combative skills.

The temple boxing school in Wu Tang is mostly acknowledged for the school's contribution to the world for the three internal styles of Tai Chi Chuan, Ba Qua and I Shing Yie. Wild boar is a specific style of boxing that the Wu Tang Monastery is named after. The Shao Lin styles practiced in this boxing school relates to all the movements of a wounded wild boar and the Shao Lin practitioners of Wu Tang fighting closely resembles the angry boar.

A complete horse riding stance in practice or combat has a variety of the low postures that are used by the fighters in offense or defense. What makes the training in the Chinese arts very hard and torturous are the very low and deeply planted to the ground horse stances while the upper body maintains an upright position. All forms are done that way in Wu Kung Kun Tao relative to the practice of the Shao Lin boxing schools.

The high kicks and lower kicking techniques in Kun Tao can be traced back to Tan's leg maneuvers. Highly noticeable for the many diversities in a variety of fighting styles, they relate directly to the Tan Tu'l or springy leg style of the boxing art and the low han forms. Named for its kicking and leg trapping, the influencing origins were named after the famous Shao Lin boxer Tan. Later he added on a greater variety of leg techniques to his art.

Tan was a poor farmer and came to the rescue of the Northern Shantung Temple boxing school. His appearance at the monastery made him aware that the iron skin style fighters were superior in combat with their deadly attacks. They could withstand the penetrating blows and kicks of the Northern Shantung fighters. Tan then created his Tan Tu'l boxing art specifically to counter the iron skin techniques, out of compassion for the Shantung boxers.

Tai Chi Chuan, the grand ultimate fist art, was practiced to understand the internal breathing arts of yoga better. It was combined with the practice of Shao Lin movements in combat. This internal art went through formidable changes in the last 1500 years. The art really began to flourish in the Chin village of China.

The healing art aspect in training T'ai Chi gives the student an understanding of rooting and in finding his timing. Through slow practice, one actually becomes faster. There are four forms of Tai Chi styles and the most known is the Yang style. Created by the Yang family, the art is twofold – the martial art and the healing art. The Chin style of Tai Chi is still practiced in the village in China. There is little difference in the practice between the two arts. The Chin style is faster and more aggressive, while the Yang form is more relaxed. Students in both arts train in the same forms, 108 long postures and 88 short postures.

A rare system of Shao Lin is the Fut Ga fighting art and is known as the art of assassins for its brutality in deadly strikes. The Shao Lin practitioners in Fut Ga had the responsibility to guard the secret books of the three internal arts hidden in the Wu Tang Temple. I Shing Yie is a forearm blasting and hitting art and a practitioner of I Shing moves in on an opponent like an unstoppable freight train.

Consistent with principles of the iron palm art, I Shing Yie becomes an art of powerful devastation when a palm iron strike is unleashed on a human body. A great pioneer of the iron palm in the US is Sigung Al Novak who still resides in Northern California. He once taught in his East Wind Gung Fu Kwoon in Oakland, California.

Most masters of I Shing Yie die young, without adding the practice of Tai Chi and Baqua to their training in order to balance out too much of the external martial arts. When the three internal arts are combined together in one force for combat, the art becomes a mauling machine by an exponent through the practice alone. The spiraling movements instantly out the lower body posture creating a severe internal penetrating power drive against an opponent's vital organs. Most Wu Kung fighters combined Shao Lin movements with the skills of the three internal arts together. With their agile, quick exchange in fast movements they were able to strike an opponent with minimum force and deliver a deep internal penetrating strike or touch that caused internal death. The cause of death is through manipulation of the blood stream with the intent action of an internal boxer.

Unique as they were, my three teachers could be considered as one of the best Kun Tao exponents that came to settle in the Dutch East Indies. As individuals they were all business to the outside world. Within the circle of their households, they were both fatherly and harsh as teachers. Expectations were high when training under these three great men. Chosen disciples were in for a duration of heavy labor efforts. Standards of a Hakka Kun Tao environment involved learning and practicing Wu Kung by experiencing arrogance, brutality, physical torture, mercilessly expressed energy all for the good of a physically inclined discipline. Every chosen student was considered a disciple. Once the candidate was elected, they were on their way to become a learned practitioner.

I have always been in favor of my training, despite the harsh treatment during my educational endeavor while learning the combative system. I was one of their best recipients of their training despite their taking me as a weakling as a student. I will always carry their spirits on the open palm of my hand, my devoted loyalty in thanks will be the grace of my soul. Without those who taught me, I would not be the individual I am today!

Typical in Kun Tao training when three masters were involved, a student had to abide himself of understanding why he was studying Shao Lin boxing in the first place. Tan Tong Liong was my first Chinese Shao Lin boxing master. He was the most energetic of the three teachers and feared by other fighters during his time. He was very challenging and dared other combatants to try him out when they crossed his path. He often scared me by losing his temper as he did with another Chinese man. My teacher was cheated out of some money by the man who sold an old cow for a young domestic bovine that he was supposed to have butchered for Master Tan. According to the man, it was the frozen carcass of a young slaughtered cow hanging in his cooled room. When my teacher noticed something, he started to rip the frozen carcass to pieces and with a few torn out ribs he held in his hands, showed the Chinese merchant who brittle an old cow looks. Master Tan broke the ribs with a quick motion of his two fingers and penetratingly twisted the broken bones into his hands. The Chinese merchant, without hesitation, gave back the money to my teacher and left in a hurry.

The Hakka people were nomadic tribes that came through outer and central Mongolia and first settled in Tibet. For thousands of years these nomads were forced to move from place to place and from continent to continent. They were in constant defense from outsiders who intruded in their lives. As unwanted people and being prosecuted everywhere, the nomadic tribesmen and their families, called the Hakka settlers, had a hard life and were always forced to defend their social lives and business ventures. As oppressed people, the Hakka tribesmen created their own means for self defense and established their very own fighting arts.

No surprise at all, the Hakka people became a very closed society open only to Hakka people. They threw out outsiders and were great in trade and in business and were very successful. Colorful in arts, clothing, poetry, music, cooking and aggressive combat systems, the Hakka tribesmen influenced the best of the boxing arts in the most noted Shao Lin monasteries in China. Much of their roots they left behind can be traced back to the Wu Tang Temple.

My father teachers were all Hakka in heart and soul. They kept to themselves and were aggressive in training and in fighting. Even the Chinese themselves had no compassion for the Hakka people of Mongolian descent. They were pushed out of Northern China and through Canton. Large scale Hakka tribes made with mass migrations to most parts of Southeast Asia and other parts of the world, making their entrances.

They went everywhere throughout the open spaces of the world to settle and to build a future. Many of them came to the Hokien region of South China and were called foreigners. They had to travel over rugged terrains and fought other tribes to stay alive. Many of the Hakka people settled over the length of the Indonesian islands over hundreds of years and influenced the Indonesian natives with their culture, customs and traditions.

Clearly shown through these illustrations are the three figures of Chen Tai Ji, Wu Kung Kun Tao and Tai Keh. Their inheritance from Shao Lin boxing is apparent with the postures. The hand and foot placements are opposite in technical meaning for their appropriate positioning of the body. The Tai Ji is the only internal boxing art. The two others are considered internal–external combative systems.

PART 8
COMPREHENSION OF KUN TAO

Buk Chin was the internal boxing master who enjoyed fighting big sailors. Aside from working and training, street combat was his favorite pastime. In size, the man was short and stocky. He was the complete opposite of Tong Liong, who was slender and muscled. When challenged by another master, Buk Chin would move in like a bullet and fight with quick encounters. He ditched his opponents' strikes or kicks with ease and returned each of his opponent's attacks as a force against himself.

Combined with his heavily muscled forearm blows, Buk Chin would land each of the punishing strikes against an adversary's anatomical region and send his challenger spinning to the ground. A well timed counter would penetrate a blood vessel. Just a soft touch of his fingertip would cause a delayed death days later from the touch strike.

Willem Chang was a huge Northern Chinese. Tall with a bull's neck, broad shoulders, and heavy set, he could move with lightening speed. Noted for this practice of the Northern fighting arts of Kwantung and Shantung boxing, he emphasized his art on the I Shing Yie hitting art of Fa Ching. The master stood 6'7" and weighed 380 pounds, which was all muscle.

When we took long walks to the city, we sometimes stopped to watch martial arts demonstrations done by experts of different Pentjac Silat styles. What amused him most was the Tukang Mentjak players who were showing their Kabangan. A Tukang Mentjac is someone who is fully trained in the fighting dance on the drum beat of a specific style. One thin Silat layer caught his eye and I, too, was impressed with the dancing skills of the man.
I knew that this thin man could be deadly in combat.

Willem Chang asked me in a whisper about the thin Silat player. He asked if the man was capable of fighting that way. I answered my huge teacher that I wasn't sure, to prevent myself from getting into trouble for a wrong answer. Knowing what my teacher could do if he wanted and what he was capable of doing, especially in anger, I looked at him and saw a bull of a man beside me. The Silat player looked like a toothpick in front of us.

Once during a practice session with my large teacher, who often scared me to death, he flattened an eight inch thick bamboo pole with his eagle talon. He grabbed and squeezed the pole with his eagle technique. I made a promise to myself that if I ever had to confront a Shao Lin Master like him, I would try to run very fast and shoot him with a 50mm gun. Of course, big men also know how to run faster than smaller guys.

The Kun Tao training I did receive from my three honorable teachers has saved my life in uncountable moments when I came close to being harmed. When someone kills out of self defense or just for the sake of killing someone, it shows their standards of humanistic gestures as a passion for hatred or a passion for love. They amount to the same thing.

What they taught me has always been a priceless possession and a meaningful essence in understanding the "way" to become one with nature. Through all the hard work, I developed a comprehension to see spiritually the path I took for achieving my life's goal of being a coach and teaching others the values in martial arts training. The wonderful people I have coached became (mostly) excellent practitioners and knew themselves better as people.

The job of guru or coach is plain and simple. It is dealing with people on an individual basis. You need to put yourself in the other guy's shoes. You give the best of yourself from within and have no expectation for any return of physical or spiritual comfort. There are no expectations when dealing with people. After all, the human race is just as unpredictable as a savings account and ends up with a bouncing check.

What I was most able to get out of all the severe and punishing training from my teachers was not only the physical, but the second nature of mental behavior. Their training paid off in my later life and I was able to make sense of any environment and to "read" people's minds. The Kun Tao training made me physically healthier and more comprehensive in what I actually do in practice.

I was never up for receiving recognitions or certifications for fighting arts. Understandably, when one considers academic achievement, it is to end up with a career to progress into the future. Diplomas really make sense up to a point. After one retires, it becomes decorative wallpaper hanging on a wall or disappears into storage in someone's closet. There are still school certifications that I never wanted to receive because I never showed up for my graduation. Funny, but true, I left a diploma aboard a ship I was leaving after I fulfilled my duty in the merchant marines. The diploma was from a Dutch college for Social Studies and history. I felt that it was nothing but a hindrance to carry the wallpaper around in my suitcase.

After I left the island of Java to return to Holland, I made my three honorable teacher–masters a promise that I would try to follow in their footsteps in sharing their arts with whoever became my students. Tan Tong Lion died by an over excessive use of alcohol and it was Dutch Gin that took his life. Buk Chin passed not long after Tan Tong Liong. The last of the three masters, Willem Chang, knew it would be the last time I would see him. He told me in a soft voice, "When you go, remember the good times together and we will always be in spirit together!" He continued saying, "Go out to the world and be us and be bigger than us." I listened with tears in my eyes and fully understood after all those years in what he meant by being bigger than those who taught me in being me.

Always hoping for the best, I hope to have done my job as a coach in teaching others their Kun Tao arts. It's one of the reasons why I gave this manuscript the title My Journey of a Guru Through Time. Several years after I left my beloved island of Java, I received through an old friend the sad news that Willem Chang had died from a heart attack. I was in Holland before I immigrated to America.

With all the complexities in Chinese Martial Arts, I would like to add some illustrations about the fighting styles of Wu Kung Kun Tao. These pertain to the difference in styles between Northern and Southern Wu Kung Kun Tao and formatted with the diversity in the figure postures. To end my eighth chapter or part with my figure sketches of the Hakka figures that will, hopefully, give a broader prospective to the reader with my illustrations and my boldness in writing.

Man being sketched was a Hakka Kun Tao warrior on his way to market. He carried merchandise in his bamboo woven baskets over his shoulders.

Nothing can outdo the Chinese Martial Arts when it comes to a collection of weapons. There are more combative instruments, from large to small, than can be found in any Chinese Kung Fu school anywhere. It clearly shows how the Mongolian and Manchurian empires influenced the growth of the combative arts in China. On this page are just a few of the weapons used in Wu Kung Kun Tao.

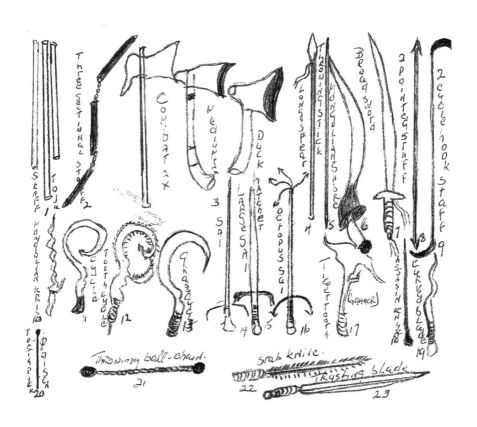

Highly influential are the very low horse stances practiced by the Hungga people used in Wu Kung Kun Tao. A low mabu fighting scene between two practitioners in a typical Wu Kung boxing style is illustrated.

Contrary to the Southern styles practiced in Wu Kung Kun Tao are the Northern sets using more of a long extended heavy hand or leg techniques. Martial Arts is practiced mostly by very large and tall individuals in the north of China and refer to their training as high mountains. This page illustrates a couple of northern Wu Kung techniques.

As time has moved on and as I look back at the past, I must consider myself a blessed man and a very lucky teacher or coach. I have been teaching here in the state of Colorado for 45 years and since then have spread the seeds of my teachers' teaching throughout most of the States and other places in the world. Since then I have touched hands with many masters and other practitioners of various fighting arts. My experiences were priceless and unmeasured with my deep appreciation.

Still thanking my closest friends, as there are actually not many, Don Ethan Miller and a few others like Dr. Andre Knutskraichen. They are my closest associates as far as martial arts are concerned. Don Miller, by far, will always remain my best friend and the very best of road partners. Despite our differences of opinion, we are all human beings with failures and successes.

In a man's life, there are many uncountable acquaintances. If a guru or coach has one loyal student or friend, he has earned the world's treasures. Sometimes one's own blood family can never be that close, aside from the person one is married to.

A reason why I add many of my illustrations to my manuscripts is for a simple and practical reason. Pictures would be too costly for printing and my own drawings allow me to explain movements in Kun Tao or Silat better since I actually practice those bodily positioning movements. My own physical practice starts at 3AM until 5AM each morning. Sitting the comfort of my living room, my mind wanders off and I think that I have lived a more passionate life through the pages of historical events. Martial Arts was always a second nature to me.

My true hero will always be the late and honorable George S. Patton. My studying my hero, I learned to understand his quotations. Not one Martial Arts master had ever accomplished what Patton and other geniuses of the past were able to do. Patton led two armies: first the 7th Army in Africa and later the 3rd Army in Europe. He was considered the greatest in the history of World War II. He captured 1, 000,000 prisoners of war with his 3rd Army. His tanks covered a distance of 80,000 square miles in France alone.

When I see even the very best of martial artists and the greatest of masters coming to me, I respect them and enjoy watching them.

I want to thank every reader who bought my first autobiography and this one. For your support in my new endeavor as I put my experiences in writing, I thank you. I fully understand that I am a butcher of language and I have to write in the context of my literary essence through the language of my spirit. It eased my heart and soul that language to me is just a composition of formatting words into sentences. Every language is going through some drastic changes almost every day.

The next three pages will be drawings of Northern Wu Kung techniques and the practice of some of the kicks that are hard to do. Then there is a fighting scene between two Hakka tribesmen during combat in the early 1900s and is self explanatory.

118

③

④

WHY IS IT IMPORTANT TO PRACTICE FORMS?

Forms in Kun Tao's tradition are pure essence for the practice alone. It relates to an old way of a traditional family combative art and can only be practiced by the members who were taught the art by teachers of the clan. Most of the clan were all Hakka families. These individuals created their own arts or combative styles. Some were directly trained under the guidance of well–seasoned exponents of any of the Shao Lin monasteries.

The Kun Tao art I have taught and trained people was influenced by body positioning in the Wu Tang traditions. Every footstep or physical expression can be traced back to the internal arts of the Wu Tang Temple. The internal arts combined into one energetic force becomes a devastating tool in actual combat. Wu Tang's tradition was known for centuries. Well trained practitioners of the temple boxing school were fierce, energetic and instant "killers" in their aggression.

My three teachers had "mercilessly" trained me to be a hardened individual for knowing my art. My gratitude to them will always be expressed through the actions of teaching, fighting and living a successful and simple life. My wife and family have always been my greatest of priorities.

Forms, therefore, can only be significant when kept to their original and purest sense of my family's art tradition. By changing any "slight" instance by any other individual who takes my teachers teaching for granted to suit their own curiosity is an Americanized version of the purity of my system. I never taught them that system. By American's kempo standards and tradition allows a student to make changes in other systems, as long as a student keeps its Kempo tradition and forms. Kempo as an Americanized system was introduced by the late and honorable Master Teacher Ed Parker. It was always a very effective and practical martial art.

Mr. Ed Parker was actually well acquainted with one of the Chinese tiger styles. The system was a great influencing source of Chow Ka. I met Mr. Parker in the early 1960's in his new dojo in Pasadena after he moved from El Monte, California. He had started to develop his Kempo basics to perfection. He looked just like Kun Tao boxer doing his art. A reason I liked Mr. Ed Parker was that most of his students knew him as the founder of American Kempo. I have known him as a Kun Tao practitioner that once came from Hawaii. All grace and appreciation goes to the late and honorable Mr. Ed Parker for creating the American Kempo system. Others that came from Hawaii went to Mr. Parker to learn American Kempo from him, then started their own system. Like anything else, they never gave Mr. Parker credit for their system.

No one Kun Tao art is like other Kun Tao styles. They are all different. My system came from the tradition and culture of my three teachers. All the forms, whether internal or external, is an opposite from other Kun Tao training in fighting, self defense or movements. Our Kun Tao art is just different when it comes to the art. What makes it opposite is my teachers. Our culture, tradition and custom is not the same as others practicing a Kun Tao fighting art. Every form, technique and martial expression has to stay specific to our Wu Kung Kun Tao in action. That is Kun Tao Silat de Thouars. It is not just the changes in what outsiders have done, which is an insult to myself and my teachers. It is their lack of understanding to Hakka tradition and a reason why they are out of my graces for good.

My expectations of individuals who are true instructors of my teachers' teaching is to keep the forms pure and maintain our old ways of tradition. Know every move and be able to explain the arts as the art was taught to you. Be consistent and always alert for a negative response from others who lack our understanding. For you who know my teachers' teaching through me will always know our philosophy and comprehend the old ways as I taught them. For you that know, be a living dictionary of the seeds I planted.

The following pages illustrate a few moves of a Northern Wu Tang form, a self explanatory use of weapons, a Southern Wu Kung form, aggressive Wu Kung actions and Hakka's nomadic tribal tradition.

123

The long staff in Wu kung

1

2

Kublan Khan
(1215 – 1294)

① Losely in his grip, was his sabre Trusted in his opponent's skull.
The Lose grip with the finger tips is greatly use, in a style
of French 15th century.

1

2

PART 9
INDONESIAN FIGHTING ARTS

My intention was first to write about my life's story in autobiographical parts; my philosophy and the journeys I experienced in episodes. Time wise those episodes were actually years, from which I had to grow up – from adolescence to manhood. Most of what I mention is of great individuals that I could hope to be. I am an individual with a lesser understanding in human endeavors.

All throughout my life's experience, I was able to understand that as human beings we are temporarily here on Earth with a Soul's mission to accomplish. None of us will ever escape death. But while alive, we may as well enjoy life's pleasures or sin or struggle to its fullest capacity. As a great president once quoted, "Don't expect from your country, what it can do for you, but give your country what you can do for your country." I follow his example and say, "Don't just take from life, but give back to life in what it has all ready given you."

Ever since my beginnings in life, I had a sincere love for wildlife and forest life. It was far greater than any of my expectations for success. Even the tiger that once chased me on the outskirts of a forest in West Java, from which I narrowly escaped from this strength and ferocity, was still a blessing in my skies for the comprehension to sense nature. The look for the large cat, and in particular the facial and eye expressions, shall always be the main actor on any of my canvasses or paper painted art. The eye expressions pertain to a generalization in the look of man and animal alike. Any artist becomes an expressionist in portraying life in art.

Of greater importance are the recollections of history, that without adding happenings of the past, not even the fiction of imaginary events or true stories can be told. As a Dutch East Indian or Indo Eurasian, I also feel the need to clarify customs and traditions of my people. As a made up race comprised of different nations, they also had made up their own fighting systems to live and survive a world of sophisticated cruelty in man's endeavor.

It is important for my offspring and students to know that Dutch Indonesian history and any of my recollected events relate to my combative arts background and the complexity of my thinking. Indonesian fighting arts first started out with the practice of individual hand to hand combat. As time evolved, matured and traditional systems were created by individuals in villages. The martial arts became favorable entities into traditional combative martial arts practices.

All throughout Indonesia's history and with the arrival of the European (primarily the English, Portuguese, Spanish and Dutch) traders between the 13th and 16th centuries, the native Indonesians were forced to defend themselves against these foreign powers of the European continent. The Europeans came for the spice trade and had in mind to colonize this rich archipelago in the middle of the Malay continent and make their territorial gain. This is the reason the sea wars were mostly between the Spanish, Dutch and English for total control of the Southwest Pacific perimeter.

Indonesia is very rich in natural resources. It is also rich is culture, customs, tradition and religion. It has been in existence for centuries despite its violent past history. Centuries before Christ came, the Manchurian, Korean, Mongolian and Chinese empires invaded the coast lines of Borneo, Celebes, Sumatra and Java for its natural resources. Much of the piracy in the waters and seas of the Indonesian islands became a source for adventuresome times in which the Southeast Asian pirates plundered and overtook merchant vessels for all their wealth.

The Europeans had already forgotten that previously the great Mongolian ruler in China, Kublai Khan, came to invade the territory of East Java with a large army. This occurred toward the end of the 12th century. Interestingly for me is the association of the Mongols and the Hakka Kun Tao art I practice. My historical point of view has been encouraged by the great Mongol Empires, the strategy of the great Khans and their dominance in battle. It is therefore of equal importance that I mention them in my manuscript since their aggression, in particular Kublai Khan's, brought him a disastrous failure in East Java and Java.

Kublai Khan was the fifth of the great Khan's of the Mongol Empire and ruled from 1260–1294. He was the founder of the famed Yang Dynasty. He was born the second son of Tolui and Songhagtani. Impressed with the Chinese philosophy for reasoning, he hired Confucian advisors for his court in Cambalue, now known as Beijing. At the request of one of his brothers who reigned over another empire, Kublai Khan took on the job as an administrator in the Song Dynasty at the age of 30. Kublai Khan managed to keep the Mongol Empire together, even during stressful times when there was a revolt in Mongolia. He aligned himself with the strong Mongol armies and other neighboring kingdoms sympathetic to his strong motivation to restore confidence in his empire. Even Marco Polo became one of his business associates in his trade with Venice. Kublai Khan, grandson of Genghis Khan, died not long after he came back from his defeat in East Java and Japan.

MORTAL COMBAT IN PENTJAC SILAT

Most of the fighting styles over the length of the Indonesian Islands was created during the conflicts of battle among the Indonesians themselves and European traders. By experiencing the European boxing and fencing skills, the Indonesians adopted the blended mix of Western combat and Southeast Asian fighting arts into their own methodology of physical arts for self defense.

The Europeans were always the warriors from the North. They were constantly combating each other through conflicts of war to conquer and invade each others' country on land and to dominate the sea with their Navies. Europeans had never known peace at any time in history.

When they started to explore and sent out excursion trips through the geniuses of countries like Italy, Spain, Holland, Great Britain and Portugal they found sea routes and became ship builders. Their uncountable sea wars were part of the discoveries of the African, European, Asian, and Australian and Great American continents. A great group of explorers came out of Scandinavia, mainly the Vikings. They discovered Holland by sailing through the rivers and canals of the Rhine in the first century.

An era in which fencing techniques were improved in modern combat was developed in the 14th and 17th centuries, when countries were at war for dominance of the sea. Piracy in the Caribbean waters was, perhaps, an example of when pirates of different nationalities fought each other. During combat, the fencers started to develop physical tactics and better footwork in movements. The foil, saber, sword and use of the combination dagger and sword was fiercely adopted in a greater sense.

Most of the crew members on the pirate ships were experienced medieval combatants and lusted for blood. They fought for survival and hoped to conquer others. Pirates were one of the best contributors to the art of fencing. Their frontal launching or "direct" piercing technique penetrated the stomach of an opponent in less than a second.

Piracy on the high seas was always an existing factor in society's Deswell fare. From thousands of years ago until today, there is a risk of astronomical loss on goods, property and lives and affects many nations in the world. Governments were faced with increasingly greater numbers of privately owned vessels of their specific countries being pirated at sea for huge sums of money.

The Chinese, Koreans, Japanese, Vietnamese, Cambodians, Indonesians and Philippine pirates were a living nightmare for fishermen and sailors on cargo vessels. Boats were constantly seized, attacked and robbed of their possessions, then the crew was slaughtered. When there was no ship to be plundered, those pirates turned against each other. This was long before the Europeans thought of building ships to cross oceans.

An interesting observation worth mentioning is how systems that were intended strictly for self defense turned into very aggressive fighting arts over a span of two thousand years. This happened in Indonesia because the Chinese had started to make ships and canons that coincided with their invention of gun powder. Their highly trained armies began to conquer other territories outside China between 4500 BC – 900 BC).

Even before Alexander the Great, Chinese armies had already invaded South Korea, Thailand, Vietnam, Cambodia, Malaysia and the city of Palembang in Sumatra. China, for ages in history, always had to struggle and through wars created several of its Dynasties.

The Han, the Ming and the Chin were Dynasties that actually created cultural wealth and very diverse martial arts. Warriors had to perform and demonstrate in front of the Emperor their highly trained skills in actual combat. This game of chess was played on a huge scaled Chess board and whoever was playing the game would tell a guard for the awaiting participant when he was ready to move. The one that fell had to die, just as he would on the battlefield. It was offender against defender and the defense had to do more than just fall. Combat on a chess board was the focus of interest for the Emperor. When the defender won the contest, the offender was killed and replaced.

China had conquered more territories than Alexander the Great did. The Chinese were very influential by educating the nations they controlled in literacy, business, commerce, and pottery and other artwork. When the Chinese left Sumatra, they left behind their treasures of art, pottery and silk weaving, which we know as batik weaving today. Indonesian puppetry was also influenced by the Chinese and can be most strongly seen in the Japanese and Korean cultures, particularly in their gardening, weaponry, watercolor painting and tea ceremonies.

Indonesian martial arts found its beginnings, when looking back in time, during the mass migrations of people from Southeast Asia and China that settled in the archipelago. This occurred 4000 years ago. With the settlement of the people with different cultures, customs and traditions came prosperity and progress.

Through commercial expansion of the Han Dynasties of China in the first century BC, came progress in technology and an upsurge in economical developments in world history. A remarkable historical observation was the literary and archaeological achievements made first by Asian scientists and, centuries later, the Europeans. The increase in production from nomads to nomads, and later country to country, did not happen overnight.

The most important progress in technology and mercantile development was in the progress that led to military diplomacy and the organization of armies. Most of the political unification in the Southeastern Countries and Indonesian Archipelago came via the efforts of China in the second and first centuries BC.

With the development of trade and politics, it is no surprise that the nations that settled in the Indonesian Islands progressed in their methods and skills in armed and unarmed combat. The development of organized modern fencing schools began to flourish in Europe in the later part of the 14th century. By this time, the Indonesians were well versed and their armies trained in the fencing arts.

Many forms of combative arts found their beginnings with individuals in villages. Later, conflicts and battles were fought between different villages in both armed and unarmed combat. It was in the nature of the native Indonesians to be aggressively combat oriented.

Going through the pages of World History is like revolving door to both the past and the future. It can bring up questions that relate to how nations came into existence and how wars were the created for economic expansion for man's greed. Politics, in some ways, pertains to the venture of man and can be compared to a stock exchange on Wall Street. It is constantly changing with the moods and attitudes of investors.

Indonesia's history has a very interesting background in business, trade and cultural exchanges. Over thousands of years, the martial arts expressions were all similar as time passed. It went through everlasting changes that are truly comparable to Wall Street. One side focused on what money is worth and the other focused on techniques for improving conditions.

History remains a very important part of my writing. It is my window of self expression. It is how I see changes in martial arts and how the expansion of economics has to do with creative thinking in martial expression. Through interacting with others, martial arts has become a socialized commodity and is not necessarily a means of self defense – not while there are guns around.

I would like to continue about the periods in history that reflect Indonesia's history on a grand scale and for each time period the changes in culture, combat, and art. These changes indirectly affected Indonesia's martial arts expansion.

The six Chinese Dynasties (Wu, Eastern Chin, Sung, Liang and Chen) were always very ambitious when extending their boundaries to the Yunnan, Kweichow, Hunan, Kwangsi, Kwantung and the northern center of modern Vietnam. During the 5th century, warriors of the Sung Dynasty had traveled extensively and fought hard battles against many underdeveloped tribes in the Malay Peninsula. They established martial arts centers and aided various tribes in organizing armies the length and breadth of Southeast Asia.

It was in the 3rd and 4th centuries when more forceful kingdoms began to enter into successful empires in Indonesia. China previously had in mind to colonize the Indonesian Archipelago for its own territory and expansion because of its rich resources. Chinese world expansion with Iran, the Middle East, and Java and allow the spread of Hinduism in those regions of the Indian Ocean. Foreigners from Southeast Asia and the Indian Ocean (the Vietnamese, Cambodians, Indians, Indonesians and Iranians) introduced Buddhism to the Chinese world. Over thousands of year, Indonesian natives with their own culture, traditions and customs became one of the most feared and savaged battle raged people the world has ever known.

During the 13th century AD, the development of economic expansion for Indonesia was done through the efforts of Gadja Mada, the foreign minister of the Majapahit Empire (1331–1364). It was a time when the Empire started to lose control. Gadja Mada stepped in and saved the Empire from further destruction. The "old" Empire was located on the basin of the Kediri region in East Java. It came to an end in 1478 to 1520. This was the greatest empire and considered an era of the Golden Age in the Malay Peninsula.

Since the arrival of European traders beginning in 1596 until the end of the era in 1948, nations inhabiting the Indonesian Archipelago had to combat politics and poverty. Dutch corporations badly exploited the native Indonesian workers for nearly 360 years. After having survived centuries of war within their social structure, the Second World War and their own war for independence from the Dutch, the Indonesian combative systems became highly sophisticated. They were a mix of European fighting arts, Dutch boxing and fencing, Chinese organized forms and the purity of Indonesia's own island flavor.

From a historical point of view, I am quite skeptical about some written articles and oral stories from several of the Dutch Indonesian Pentjac Silat exponents. They traveled to the USA and taught their combative systems here. Their skills and martial arts practices were, in my point of view, the highest caliber. Their ideas in which they claimed imaginative commentaries of Indonesian natives unable to practice their Pentjac Silat Arts during Dutch Colonial times were to-

tally misleading and false. These individuals even had their students believing in their fantasy to make things interesting.

If a son of a Dutch Governor was practicing in a Kampong (village) and trained in Pentjac Silat, what was up with the ideas of these individuals? The late and honorable Dutch Indonesian Lieutenant General, formerly a general in the Dutch Colonial Army was practicing a system of Solok in Ache and knew Pukulan. His name was Lieutenant General Gerardus Johannes Berenschot.

Even the Dutch Governor General over the East Indies, A.W.L. Tjarda van Starkenburg Stachouwer of Dutch noble descent had practiced Pukulan of Djakarta style. He was Governor General until the Japanese invasion in May, 1942.

On the contrary to some people's beliefs, the Dutch never interfered with the nations of Indonesia and their cultural traditions. That includes the practice of Pentjac Silat and their Kembang Dance.

KEMBANGAN: A TRADITION IN SILAT

The old Indonesian Kabana Arts (Flower Dance) is a dance performed by a well practiced exponent of his specific Silat style. By tradition, it was demonstrated on tournaments or festivities. The dance was stylish and full of grace with the exactness in movements on the drum beat. Experienced observers would notice and detect which style of Silat is shown and how much the man actually knew about his own art. A well seasoned and knowledgeable practitioner of a style is quickly acknowledged by his skill and explosive actions. It can have deadly results when done with intent when an opponent was hit or struck by his energetic force of brutality.

15   16   17   18   19

152

25

24

26

27

153

28

29

PART 10
A MODERN ERA IN SILAT'S TRADITION

Most of the more modern Pentjac Silat arts were created between the eighteenth and nineteenth centuries. The term "Pentjac" relates to a Southern Chinese dialectic expression for training in punching, blocking and kicking. Starting out first with the term "pung," it means to block. "Tja" relates to a systematic effort in which punching is used in different ways. "Te" is a way in which a practitioner trains in his particular method of kicking and sweeping. The origin of the word goes back to Hokien's dialect and sounds like "pung," "tja" and "te."

After a period of many years, Indonesian natives added the slang expression from Southern China and added their to their own vocabulary the expression for basic training as "Penjac." Literally, it means how blocking is done. Accordingly it adds hitting and kicking as part of the curriculum relating to a system of basic structure. After a student has fully trained in the basics (Pung–Tja–Te), he advances to the knowledge of Si–La and Te. It pertains to the Hokien dialect as refinement in skills. Like the term "Pentjac" as a basic practice, "Si La Te" becomes Silat in Behasa.

Concerning the Island of Java alone as a subject in relation to many of the variable Silat styles, the oldest systems of the Indonesian Arts are still practiced in East and Central Java. The natives in those regions of the Island have always maintained their culture and tradition in practice. Their fighting arts date back to the Sultanate of Matarm of the ninth century East Java. Practitioners from Central and East Java never changed their culture in practice. They were always a highly furious blade fighting people with or without weapons. Their tradition goes back to the Sultanate that was a Hindu and Buddhist Empire and the last of the great East Javanese kingdoms that reigned over a large territory. The warriors of that era never practiced martial arts with Jurus or Langkas. Their training consisted of mostly low ground fighting and a lot of leaping out of positions on the ground.

Practitioners of Silat in West Java were mostly relying on their training of more organized systems and in the practice of Jurus and Langkas, Pantjars, Seliwas and worked off platforms. Most of the known West Javanese Silat systems, like Ci Mande, Serak, Ci Kalong, Monjet Bogor, and Silat Betawi, can easily be traced back to the

Chinese Kung Fu boxing arts. This is one of the reasons why they are more structured than the Silat Arts from Central and East Java.

The systems were created by Mas Ibung Kahir concerning the Ci Mande "Tulen." Serak was founded by Pak Serak. Not much thought was given to it at any time that Silat Monjet Bogor (Monkey Art of Bogor) should be credited to a certain Petit de Roy of Djakarta of the 1920's. A question I have asked myself many times over was, "If Mas Kahir and Pak Serak taught their systems to their lineage holders (Mas Djoet and Atma) in the beginning of the nineteenth century, how anyone can claim the Art of Serak came through the practice of Silat during the Majapahit Empire in the thirteenth century?" Whoever made these claims must have spent a lot of time in Disney World and was taken in by tales of Snow White and the adventures of Bambi.

Pentjac Kendang Silat was a system from West Java that was created by two distinguished martial arts practitioners who lived on the outskirts of Bandung. After observing a tournament in a village in Bogor, the two men (Mas Sardjono and Pak Atjo) were impressed with a fighter who used Ci Mande fighting skills combines with Serak's forward movements. The fighter had capabilities that others in the same arena outside the village were unable to comprehend. When they tried to counter his attack, the fighter was more aggressive and agile. He had quick, evading steps and could move in with ease on an opponent and swept most adversaries off their feet. The same fighter was also a Hokien Kun Tao practitioner and this was, most likely, the evidence behind the strength of his fighting skills.

After watching and admiring the fighter, Sardjono and Atjo developed their fighting art. They art they created was named after the Kendang Tournament. The two masters used lots of the Kun Tao hitting and striking arts combined with the Ci Mande system of side stepping and the forward linear movements of Serak.

The upright position that we find in Serak came directly out of a Chinese fighting art we know as I Shing Yie. It is also noted for the combination of hitting and elbow striking as a method of punching. In Indonesia, the postures are still practiced, such as the very low horse riding stance. When the art was developed by two gurus, Atjo and Ardjono, they called their newly found system Pentjac Kendang Silat.

Their art, which I highly treasure for it's simplicity in fighting, has only two other form sets. The most basic is Juru Satu, or the number one hand and leg set. This is followed by a short internal set (a Pakua oriented art), Langka Dua (leg form number two) and Langka Tiga (leg and hand pattern set number 3). The whole short system of Pentjac Kendang Silat comprises more Chinese low and deep horse stances and was, realistically speaking, designed as a fast fighting style. All three forms have influences of Ci Mande, Serak and other arts and with many versatile fighting techniques.

Hakku Kun Tao is highly noticeable in Kendang Silat as a strong basic style. Each set has totally different leg maneuvers and are opposite each other. What is unique in this system is how the sets relate to each other as a complete system. For instance, in order to practice Langka 3, the hand pattern 3 comes out of Djuru 1 and Langka 2 combined. The two masters were actually geniuses to have created the style. They will always have my eternal thanks for teaching me their martial art as a great basic style to practice.

JURU SATU

The very first set of Pentjac Kendang Silat, a set I have taught to many individuals in many places, is probably the most practiced form in my system. The hand pattern set is easy to learn and, as a basic, is great to practice.

ILLUSTRATIONS OF JURU SATU.

Special consideration should be given to my grandfather, Jan deVries, who was my maternal grandfather. Jan was the son of a Dutch land developer who once owned a law firm in New York City. It was here on the East Coast were he met his wife, my great grandmother. Mary Tuford was a beautiful, enchanting and very charming Black lady of African descent.

Mary Tuford was the daughter of a preacher and grew up in a Christian family. The whole Tuford family was handsome and it still amazes me that black really is not black. It can be distinguished in a row of colors between light brown and dark brown. Charcoal black or shoe polish black does not relate to any skin color, and most certainly not in my book. I see things from an opposite side of the fence from most people. Most people lash out at individuals who do not look the same as they do.

My great grandparents left New York City on a steamer for the Dutch East Indies. It must have been during the Civil War era. Being a realist myself, I am sure that the brothers de Thouars fall under the category of third generation Americans.

Blessed as we were, my other great uncles and aunties who came out of the de Vries and Tuford marriage, ended up like nobility. The men became generals, governors and even Dutch ministers. They reminded me of a relationship that once existed between Thomas Jefferson and Sally Hemings, except my great–grandfather married Mary Tuford.

As offspring from the marriage of the Dutch de Vries and the native American of African descent, their children and grandchildren made East Indian and Dutch history as high ranking military officers, Dutch government officials and successful merchants. They were also social contributors to the European economic society.

My grandfather, Jan de Vries, bought a tea plantation and had three different spouses. All were native Indonesian women. My mother was the third oldest and she had three brothers and four sisters. The last of the de Vries girls was my Aunt Julia, who died a few years back in Kona, Hawaii. My family there, Dr. Behati Mershant and I were visiting her in a rest home in Kona before she passed.

What was unique about my grandfather was the way he lived his life as a half breed in a social environment in the Dutch Colonial time. I can only describe him from pictures, stories told from family and friends, and how he actually ended his life which was unnecessary.

My brothers and I did not know our grandfather, Jan de Vries.

Through my imagination, I often looked at old pictures and listened to interesting stories from the recollections of our uncles and Jan's old friends. Some of his friends, white Dutch, Dutch Indonesians and some native Indonesians who served in the Colonial Army were unable to remain in Indonesia and had to leave their native country. Unfairly judged by man, they were considered to be traitors. It is hard to imagine that without his presence, the art of Pencak Silat Serak would not have been practiced in the de Vries and de Thouars families.

Our family was quite large and Jan had other brothers and cousins. All were Silat practitioners. There were eight de Vries men who enjoyed the taste of combat in the streets or outskirts of a rough city. They were always lusting for the stain of blood in healthy fighting, like the old days in America. Somehow my family's heritage reminded me of Jim Courbet's family and his bouts with John Sullivan. The great John L. Sullivan must have also studied some Chinese Kung Fu, just by looking at his physique and watching him pose standing in his I Shing Yie stance.

My remembering the life of my grandfather, it will hopefully bring some invaluable information for the ones who have studied under any of my cousins in Holland, my brother Maurice, or any of the three of us brothers here in the United States and other places in the world. Many people that had never "truthfully" known the background of the de Thouars and the de Vries families told incorrect stories about my family. Most of the misinformation came through exaggeration and assumptions. In every family circle, families fight. No matter what, we brothers – Paul, Victor and I – have had our share of "spitball" throwing contests, provided there are no outsiders involved.

My written recollection concerning my grandfather and his martial arts experiences and endeavors in the use of Serak and Kun Tao in combat were true stories. Because my grandfather was a very interesting man, it was worth every effort to mention him.

Who was Jan de Vries and how did he leave behind such a large boot print for his offspring to follow can easily be measured through our compassion and our vision of him as our idol. By observing the grin behind his small mustache on a picture, Jan really was a handsome man. He had the looks of Errol Flynn, the great screen idol of the past. He was also adventurous and broke any rule or regulation in behaviorism in Dutch Colonial society. He was full of "spice" and always had the lust for a good fight against anyone, large or small. Size did not matter to him. He mostly fought other European men in the country club he belonged to. During his time, boxing was not called boxing. They referred to boxing as the manly sport of pugilism. In pugilism, everything goes and was allowed to be used, from elbows to knees. Everything but eye gouging was allowed.

Most of all, my grandfather had a keen eye for beautiful women and enjoyed health conversations and sports. In the country club, he often accepted challenges from other men who were jealous of losing a female they were courting. The white Dutch did not like half breeds in particular since they were not a "pure" race. It was annoying for those Colonials to see a better dancer or to see a dualistic fencer walk dashingly away with a most luscious blonde who had otherwise been the focus of their interest. Challenges among the men became an even greater pastime and Jan de Vries, the way he was, enjoyed the moment in his conquest for physical combat. Through the focus of attention an eye witness saw one of his challengers being chased by my grandfather. My grandfather fought furiously like a tiger in a box and was ready to spank his adversary like a little kid.

Ever since Jan learned the fighting arts in self defense, he became well versed in Chinese Kun Tao, fencing and boxing. He was often in trouble with his mother, Mary Tuford, and my great grandfather de Vries for neglecting his school studies. Jan wanted to see the grass on the other side of the fence, even when it meant receiving physical punishment at the hands of his parents for his lack of interest in education.

When Jan was in his twenties, he began to assume his career on plantations as a tea grower and later became a successful tea plantation owner. When he met Mas Djoet, who had worked for the Dutch East Indian Railroad Company, he also met his future father–in–law. Both men trained together in several native Pentjac Silat styles. My own father–in–law, Carl C. Deems, was also my Ci Mande teacher. His father was in the service of the same railroad company as Mas Djoet.

Mas Djoet was a greatly accomplished guru in Serak and taught Jan the art. My grandfather's love for Serak was exactly like my lust for doughnuts and sweets. He became a hardened and diverse fighter and well known for using Serak successfully in combat.

He loved the art to much that he dedicated his free time staging huge Silat tournaments on weekends behind his plantation home. The home Jan and my mother's family lived on was a five acre lot surrounded with luscious greens and located in a dense forest. Tea, rubber and coffee plantations were mostly located in mountainous regions of West Java. My grandfather's plantation was above Garut in West Java. The scenery of his endless blooming tea fields with the sweet aromatic smell of tea plants surrounded his home in the forest.

When Jan staged his Pentjac Silat tournaments, they kept going for three days and nights. Every Pentjac Silat practitioner from family, friends and those from different villages came to participate. It was just like a traditional festivity. It was full of excitement for the participants watching the Kendang fights and to listen to the drumbeat solos as a sign for the participant to increase or decrease movements.

Most interesting with the Kendang fights was when a young maiden gracefully displayed her inviting dance movements for any of the men. She placed a piece of silk cloth in her blouse that hung loosely for the experienced Kendang fighter to quickly snatch away with the gentle tips of his fingers. The lucky "snatcher" had to be prepared for battle because someone else would jump in and try to take away the silk cloth for the honor of the young woman. If both were unsuccessful for some reason, each performed their Kendang dance. Each man tries to encircle each other in the smoothness and agility of the movements, as the drum solo encouraged both men to start combat.

In Kendang tournaments, the combat was very interesting, as I had also participated in my time. The one who tumbled down or was swept to the ground through the skill and technique of his opponent was declared the loser. For a champion in the olden days or golden days of Silat, they had to keep fighting one opponent after another until he was able to maintain his ground or became so exhausted he could no longer participate.

The tournaments held by my grandfather were like a family event and the noise of the drums could be heard for miles. The other white Dutch plantation owners considered these to be a low life stage with barbaric events. None of them ever approached my grandfather. My grandfather died after he came back from a party at the Dutch club drunk one evening. He fell down in his living room and slept on the cement floor. The severity of his frozen lungs and hypothermia ended the colorful life of my grandfather.

I was always the skinniest kid in the family. My brothers were all large bodied and there was much to say about their physical strength. They were all after the physique of my dad who stood 6'8" and weighed 288 pounds, all solid muscle. He also practiced boxing and Silat. I trained myself in running faster than any of them.

In reminiscing about my grandfather, I discovered how important the martial arts history of my family is. Serak as a West Javanese fighting art was a thoughtful idea for explaining my point of view on the subject. No one knows the exact relation in practice between Ibung Kahir, the founder of Ci Mande and Pak Serak as the creator of Serak and how the pertain to each other in their practice.

We know from an historical point of view that Ibung Kahir was a horse trader and traveled extensively throughout the region of West Java. He settled near Tji Andjur, a mountain village, a married a woman in the village. After he settled in the village, the villagers renamed it Ci Mande Village.

Ibung Kahir was taught an art called Ba Qua by a Southern Chinese man. It could easy be noticed in the circular and evasive movements of the art he invented and later referred to as Ci Mande. Many influencing factors of Kun Tao have been integrated to bring flavor to the art's benefit. For instance, the hardening of the arms and body traces back to China's Kung Fu Iron Skin training. Even the Belur rubbing smelly oil for muscle and bone healing came from studies of Chinese internal medicine. It is most unlikely that Ibung Kahir had killed his Chinese teacher after having studied from the Chinese man.

No one was able to recollect any historical event if Pak Serak was a student of Ibung Kahir or not. It was just assumed that way. Ci Mande, Ci Kalong and Serak were always three Pencak Silat systems that were closely related with only a specific way in which every art has different practices in training. This, of course, was purely out of my own perspective in how I perceived the intent for addressing this issue. These have been topics of conversations since the art was created.

No one knows where Pak Serak learned his art form or where he studied, but he was a real figure in the world of Silat in West Java. As far as I am concerned, he was from in the city of Cheribon and trained a few good men in his art of Serak.

Some of the most known exponents and gurus in his art were Guru Marun and Mas Djoet for Ci Mande Silat was Raden Atma. They were around at the same time. It may be of interest to instructors and students under Pendekar Paul, Ma Ha Guru Victor and yours truly to visualize our brother's situation. When my uncles de Vries were studying Serak from Mas Djoet and Marun, my father in law was training at the same time under Atma in the art of Ci Mande Silat. Pak Serak and Ibung Kahir were both born in the late 1800's.

My grandfather, who was an excellent fighter and practitioner in Serak, lacked the patience for teaching and introduced his nephews, Uncle John, Freddy and Ness to Mas Djoet. He trained them and six others in the art. While Pak Serak, on the other hand, taught other individuals like Lie Gai van der Groen, Groenewald, Sultan Hamid IIfrom Pontianak, Uncle Eddy de Vries and a few others. Some later became highly respected gurus in West Javanese Silat.

Evaluating Silat as a fighting art is unique on its own and seeing it was an experienced Kun Tao and Silat practitioner, I can easily detect the influences of Pakua, I Shingyie and other Kung Fu combined in the movements of the style. Below are some old photo copy shots from Uncle John and Uncle Ventje practicing Serak in Uncle John's studio. Uncle John is doing langkas. I also included Willem Reeders clips. All pictures were taken in Holland in 1955.

Prior to the second World War, in the late 1920's, Uncle Willem Reeders and the Uncle's John and Ventje were always practicing Serak and Kun Tao together. Underneath are a few old photos of Uncle Willem Reeders demonstrating Serak in Uncle John's school in Amsterdam, Holland in 1955.

PART 11
MY LIVELY EPISODES THROUGH TIME
(A PREFACE)

I am, most likely, totally different in my intent of writing when it comes to approaching a subject from most other distinguished writers. They are far greater than I in their language and organizational skills. For someone like me, it is most difficult to be a meticulous writer. I see only perfection as a keen object to a literary accomplishment. Not taking away an initiative for a standardized behavior of my touching the keyboard, I see languages changing daily. In a phrase, I will continue my endeavor in writing with the simplicity of my thinking. Also understanding a method in which standard English can be perceived in a more acceptable means, I only feel the comfort of my surroundings through the "hypertension" of my sugar sweets. Seemingly unperceivable, I also had great versions of examples like Don Ethan Miller, who wrote great Hollywood scripts. My constant companion when I write is WARRINER'S (a complete course in English grammar and composition) and a thick dictionary like Webster's.

The WARRINER'S book was given to me as a present by a distinguished and lovely nurse in early 1960. She was the Head Nurse for the surgical ward for the Huntington Memorial Hospital in Pasadena, California. I was employed by the same hospital as a custodian. When I spoke my English it was with a discomfort in my tone of voice. The lovely nurse was Miss Martin. She was a wonderful lady who had served during the Second World War in the Southwest Pacific theater and was one of the American nursing staff under the famous Dr. Wetzel. Dr. Wetzel worked for the Allies in Ci La Ciap, a Dutch held territory in the Indies. I am not sure if someone still remembers a movie about Dr. Wetzel before the Japanese Imperial Army seized the East Indies. Miss Martin was one of the nurses. Gary Cooper starred in the movie.

I was because of her that I got hired as a custodian. I worked for her on the second shift. She was attractive and petite, but never married. She was once engaged to an American Army officer, who fell in Bataan. You just can't imagine me as a young and healthy man in my mid twenties being around an attractive and appealing young American female who had been overseas and was experienced in the facts of life. Was I attracted to her? For sure! Was I in love with her? It was a true and scary thought. One evening Miss Martin asked me for a date so that we could talk. She wanted to help me with my English. I was somewhat embarrassed at first. Later, she brought me more into my comfort zone. I really looked forward to spending time with her.

We went on several dates to the movies, restaurants and the most classy places for ballroom dancing. She was an awesome dancer and complimented me for maintaining myself as a gentleman. She hardly felt threatened with me. I respected the lady so much, no matter what the feelings were inside me. Most of all, she was my boss and a great friend for socializing. As time moved on in my life, I needed a change in employment. Being close to a lady I began to have feelings for was going to be hard to bear in the long run. She taught me a lot in my barrier with the English language. I will always remember the little nurse from Ci La Ciap that was there for me and aided me in a difficult period of my life.

After I was hired with the Von Braun Industries as a machinist, I brought her roses on my last evening at the hospital. I told her in a caring voice, "Miss Martin, I thank you for all you did for me. I am leaving for a better future and will always remember you." I saw some tears rolling down her face and she said, "Willem, thank you for you. You will always be a part of my life. Here is the book I taught you out of, WARRINER'S English Grammar and Composition book. Always write from your heart my friend. And with this book, you will never get stuck!" When I left the hospital, tears were also rolling off my cheeks. Now forty–nine years later while writing my manuscript, my soul and feelings go out in spirit to the little nurse from Ci La Ciap. I will always be grateful to her, not for her beauty, but for her greater soul as a gracious human being.

THE GURU IN ME

When I started to teach, it was first more of a task than a pleasurable event because I lacked language and communication in how to be a teacher, coach or guru. In all sincerity, I had no clue and no experience in teaching. Because Joyce and I were married in 1964 and moved from California to Colorado, I also had no experience in dealing with American cowboys.

The year was 1965 and, as I promised my teachers, I would be a coach and teach their system. I remember the times like yesterday. I had to fulfill my destiny and start to teach my teachers' martial arts practices and "spread" their seeds into the world, so to speak. The start, however, was my place of residence in Thornton, Colorado. I gave it a lot of thought and on street corners in Denver there were many homeless people. I had no clue then that they were "a" socialites in Colorado's social living structure.

In the beginning in the early 1960's, there weren't many martial arts schools. Most were Karate, Aikido and Judo dojos. You were able to purchase uniforms or belts in Japanese gas stations. Kung Fu was still a foreign word. In particular, the arts I practiced were a total failure to even talk about. I had a very slim and thin experience in teaching Americans.

One day I had to go to the Oriental store for Joyce, which was in downtown Denver. On my way to the store, a guy and a drunk, who did not like Hispanic people confused my looks for a Mexican, despite my Southwest Pacific looks. As he approached me, he had already given me a "funny feeling" to be alert. My second nature in figuring out people had never left my soul. The man swung at me with an empty wine bottle. I just ditched his swing. It's not hard to sweep a drunk off his feet. Without a touch, the man was laid out in dreamland and resting like a baby on the asphalt street by the Oriental store.

When I came out of the store with sacks of groceries, some strangers approached me and told me, "Hey, you doing that Kung Fu stuff. I see the Green Hornet was doing that. I like to learn that dude, would you teach us?" The Green Hornet series had just started. I replied and said, "Okay," and invited them to come and see me in Thornton. I gave them my address and they came for only two Sundays. Little did I know they were hard core winos and were part of the homeless bunch. I really could not teach them anything, but supplied them with some old boxing gloves and had them go wild on each other. It was funny to see. I was eating breakfast and they were fighting each other, if one could call it fighting. They were staggering, falling and doing some really wild swinging with no understanding of combat. Joyce and I were just married and my sweet wife was so full of frustration with the winos. I ended the teacher/student relationship and never saw them again.

One year later, I started a new group with rodeo guys. They were high spirited just like the horses. I really had to fight them in order to get them to understand what I was teaching. Cowboys, I found, are some of the toughest guys. Above all, they are the best for a reality check in what works and what doesn't.

The experience I obtained in training cowboys was in one word "grand" and precisely magnificent. It was difficult, but rewarding for me to understand the American frame of mind. When you teach someone from a city, they can be considered a "softie." But a rodeo guy is an endeavor in the study of physical essence. When it comes to grappling the neck of a 15,000 pound bull riding it in a rodeo is beyond most people's imagination. It is huge and a bull is a magnificent animal in its size and strength. The neck of even the strongest man on Earth compared to that of a rodeo bull is as thin as a goose. As rewarding as the opportunity with the cowboys was, some of them are still after me. They were never aware of the broken ribs and bones I sustained from teaching those guys.

As time progressed, I was gaining an ardent reputation among tough guys for being a brutal hitting "son of a bitch." I gained much of their respect. Teaching in the late sixties and early seventies, I gained a better comprehension of my American students. I love them all!

When I was gaining more students and started to train individuals of different styles or individuals outside the state of Colorado, I found I needed to spread my teacher's seeds. I could write or explain in many chapters about myself and my experiences. But it's not fair in my opinion and does not serve my purpose for writing in an appropriate sense. After all, it can never be all about me. It also concerns the individuals who have been with me for many years. There are quite a few I could consider as my family. They are hardcore practitioners and good friends. Without them, my wife, family and practitioners I would never be me. In the best way of my feelings can be expressed, I am the guru within.

The longest one of my disciples has been with me has to be Guru Phillip Sailas. I have known the man and his family for over 40 years. He is a man I love, treasure and is actually the closest in my practice and near in what I am doing. To honor him and his everlasting friendship, I would like to share his endorsement of my manuscript with the reader.

AN EXPERIENCE OF A LONG TIME DISCIPLE

Explained in his own writing about martial arts…

I am Phillip Salias, one of Uncle Bill's senior students.
I went to the military right out of high school and became a Marine, where I was introduced to the basics of self defense. I served in Vietnam for one year. I was in the military from 1969 to 1970.

In 1972, I married and had two sons, Phillip and Andrew. My wife of four years, Christina, decided to take some self defense classes at the Denver Community School. She would come home after each class and ask if she could practice on me. I said yes not knowing what I was getting myself into. I was getting tired of getting beat up by my own wife. What she seemed to be learning interested me, so I decided to join her.

There is where I came across a man, Russel Perron, who later became my first teacher. I studied Tae Kwon Do for nine months. Later I met Earl Austin who taught me Okinawa-Te. He later became my teacher when Russel Perron left Denver and closed his school.

Mr. Earl Austin taught out of the Thornton Recreation Center. That is where I met William de Thouars (Uncle Bill), which I later had the great privilege of becoming one of his students. I started with Uncle Bill in the early 1970's. I was just amazed by what he had to teach. I have never met a man that was so gentle and humble and quiet. But when he would teach he was so explosive and full of energy. There was so much to learn, so much to see and I was always amazed by what he had to teach.

Today I am still with Uncle Bill after 40 years and I still haven't touched the surface of what he has to offer. I am eternally grateful to have know William de Thouars (Uncle Bill).

Uncle Bill, I would like to thank you for all that you have taught me and given me throughout the years. With love and my deepest respect and gratitude I thank you.

Sincerely,
Your Senior Student
PHILLIP SAILAS

MY BIG BROTHERS AND ME

Too often, what is with most people is that they take themselves too seriously and somehow over exaggerate into a passion of becoming very sensitive. When this starts to happen, a good laugh was never an appreciative issue. While I, on the other hand, never cared if someone was mad at me or made some strange remark toward me. Words usually bounced back from where it came from. Words are just words and what matters is really an advice when dealing with the human race. You may stumble on a water or food shortage, but the world will never run out of "assholes."

Living with my brothers in one place was a true adventure and a riot. My mother and three brothers, Maurice, Paul, Victor, and myself once lived in a flat in the village of Wormer in North Holland. Everything was fine, as far as I was concerned, except that all dinner table conversations between family and friends ended up in Silat discussions. Serak was above and beyond anyone's imagination. It tipped the scales away from food in such discussions.

To me, that is not the brighter side of life. Consider the subject as a humanistic inclined adventure that leads nowhere except to Serak, Serak, Serak and Serak. More appropriate issues can be addressed in a merger for an expansion of more delightful conversations as a focus of interest. Having problems with my conversations at home, I decided to pull a prankster joke on my brothers.

People in the village, especially a fat Dutch woman, felt compassion toward me since I was underweight while my brothers were so big and well nourished. I was imposing on their sympathy with the women and told them (jokingly) a story that living at home under those conditions was unbearable for me. I still laugh about the story I told the fat ladies and the villagers.

Immediately, the kind Dutch ladies were full of fear for me and wanted to know what was going on with that strange Indo family in the village. In a whisper, I told one of the ladies, very convincingly, that my brothers always deprived me of my food. That was the reason I was shaking, because I was hungry.

Soon after, the story I told the lady spread like wildfire around the village. The villagers and store owners closed their doors to my brothers. They had to travel to Amsterdam to purchase their necessities. I never meant for this to happen, but people were taking themselves so seriously. All of my life I've had the misfortune for just being a skinny runt. And I am still a skinny runt.

Finally, I corrected the mistake I made and told the mayor of the village that I was born a prankster. I explained the whole story. As a reprisal on me from the villagers, I could not purchase anything in store located in Wormer. Not that it mattered to me. I left as a Merchant Marine sailor on a trip to South America.

My mother was extremely happy for me to go overseas since I had always gotten in trouble in Holland. The Chief of Police told me that Wormer was a peaceful place until I came along. At the time I was eighteen without any common sense and the Chief of Police always told me the same thing every time I saw him. I had an excessive amount of energy and had eaten too much sugar. With all due respect to the Dutch police, I was put in a cell for a few days to cool off after I told my story.

My brother Paul and I had another adventure when we both got into the village of Wormer. After I came back from a trip, I met Paul at the Central Station in Amsterdam and we headed for home. He always bragged about how he looked like Winston Churchill and that he was always smoking cigars. It was a Friday afternoon when we boarded the train. It was February, 1954 and freezing cold in Holland.

Our walk from the station to our flat in Wormer was a solid thirty to forty minute walk. In summer, it was more of a stroll to get home. In freezing temperatures with the North Sea wind blowing against you, even the thickest clothing does not provide warmth or protection.

During our walk, Paul was persistent about wanting to take a short cut to our flat. The smoke from his cigar was torturing me. Between our flat and where we were stood a large acreage of farm land with a large herd of cattle grazing. The great idea was to take a short cut and go straight through the farmland to shorten our journey.

Passing by the grazing cows was not bad. The animals were just looking at us like we never belonged on their land. Suddenly the ground began to shake. A big unpleasant roar like noise came out of a huge bull. He stamped his legs violently on the ground beneath him and ran after us. Being the skinniest, I was running for dear life with Paul close behind. The bull was easily gaining ground on us. While Paul was running, his cigar remained in his mouth, resting on one side of his Errol Flynn type mustache. The cigar butt had burned his mustache. We were near exhaustion when we reached the wire fence that separated the farm from our flat. I easily cleared the wire with an agile leap, but Paul got stuck by his pants on the wire. The bull enjoyed the occasion and with the might of his horns picked up my bigger brother and tossed him over the fence. Paul was tough and okay, but leaned on me to help him get up the steps to our apartment.

I never saw my brother fly through the air like Superman. Sadly, there are no Silat techniques in the whole world that can have any quality of good measure to stop a 2,000 pound Dutch bull in his tracks.

PART 12
A BROADMINDED VIEW ON MARTIAL ARTS

Being in the practice of martial arts for a very long time, I would like to share with the reader my most sincere and honest opinion considering my point of view on the subject of martial arts.

Regarding my humble respect to the many masters and students I have met over the years, here in America and overseas, I could always relate to the productive time they spent training and teaching martial arts. Most of them were excellent in what they were doing. Regardless of what anyone else felt about them, I thought highly of them. They were to be commended for a job well done. A few students, through the efforts of their teachers, became outstanding examples of their teachers' intentions.

And yet, despite all the good things that evolved in the martial arts around the world, and particularly in the United States, the human race expanded with fewer points of simplicity and merged into false values in the world of martial arts. For instance, martial arts was intended to be just for self defense, but it was turned into an entertaining social environment in which it has become a wealth resource. This dominates over the purity of its origin.

The wrong of the human race is the greed for possessions. Many well trained martial artists, regardless of their style or system, found a way to please their hunger for satisfaction by creating their own systems. They thought they were the founders of new inventions.

In broadening my ventures through my intent, I would be sincere by expressing my focus of attention to the truth. Out of my own experience, I relate my findings to the "flawless" and inadequate misadventures of a few individuals. They thought they had improved to a technically superb level, but it had already been thought of by others thousands of years ago.

Uncountable numbers of grand experts in martial arts came out of the woodwork, claiming to be the best the world has to offer. This gesture alone brought a great uncertainty to the mindset of a prospective student. The student could have been an adequate candidate for any martial arts school's environment.

Much to my confusion were the rankings of the grand experts provided for themselves as a measure to strengthen their insecure mental activities in exchange for a comfort zone. It was created to secure their martial arts environment.

I was greatly amazed and amused when I saw many of the grand experts, once known to me, come up in their ranks and then expected me to humble myself in front of their students while they were on their throne. Laughing to myself, I was neither impressed nor embarrassed with their ranking. They considered themselves the Han Shi, the Shi Han, Sigung, Supreme Grandmaster, Senior Grandmaster, Grandmaster, Ma Ha Guru, Pendekar, Guru Besar – the list is endless.

When I took on the job of writing my experiences in martial arts and my escapades in life, I decided to be honest, upright and resourceful with the historical events that pertain to martial arts. History has always been a resource for exploring life and in getting to know myself in venturing into the unknown. In some instance, it is also about me and my experience. Otherwise, how can I relate myself to someone else as an individual when it concerns the human being in us.

The martial arts as a venture into life is an absolute. It is a second nature like a good or bad habit. It is an excellent idea for training hard in any fighting art. It is beneficial for one's own health and for staying physically fit. I call it longevity for living.

What martial arts really means to me is that it is a form of exercise and strictly for self defense. When someone refers to a master and how great he is, I turn around and shake my head. When someone tells me how "magnificent" I am in my art, I turn around in shame for the teachers who taught me. My job was always to plant a seed for my teachers. I have done a lot of coaching for my teachers before me. Therefore I don't have a rank, only the position of "Uncle." I made Grandmasters of my most senior practitioners after they spent many years with me. Because it was my own personal art that I taught, I spread my teachers' seed. Their job is to set forth the seed I planted.

Before I continue my writing concerning my further studies of learning Eastern Javanese Silat, I would like to share with the reader a martial arts point of view of one of my instructors, Sigung Ted Garcia. Mr. Ted Garcia is a highly talented gentleman with a diverse martial arts background. He has distinguished himself as one of my leading successors. He is also a formidable and accomplished painter, artist and illustrator.

Throughout my years of teaching, my main interest for my students was the job I left behind for them to follow. As a teacher, I had to provide and instill confidence in each of them, whether they were good or bad students. I had to give them the very best of me. While it is almost impossible to have bad students, the other side of them is always the good nature in men.

As orders come streaming in for my present book, I am coming near the end of my endeavor. I wish to thank everyone, especially my students, for all your support. It would greatly help me to cover printing costs if my reader enjoys this book in a simple language. After all it's my intent to not prove how great I am as a martial artist. What is more important is the job I have done for my teachers. I hereby thank Sigung Ted Garcia for his endorsement.

12/28/09

Since I was young, I've been practicing martial arts, and yet, after training and obtaining many high ranks in various styles, I felt something was still missing. Then, in 1993, I was introduced to BAPAK Willem de Thouars, (or as he is known worldwide, "Uncle Bill") and his Kun Tao Silat, when I quickly realized this is what I've been looking for.

Uncle Bill, with open arms, welcomed me into training with him and his seniors. I felt that day, as I do to this day, very privileged and honored to be accepted, not only into this incredible martial art, but more importantly, I was welcomed into his wonderful family.

Uncle Bill, with his endless salad bowl of knowledge, has shared so many things that have influenced my life, not only martially but personally as well. For this, I can never say thank you enough. From a simple act of how to stand and breathe to the complexity of proper angles, his techniques are extremely effective.

Uncle Bill, may your book be as fruitful and prosperous as your martial arts have been.

With the upmost appreciation and admiration, your student, your nephew and your friend,

TED GARCIA
Evergreen, Colorado

FROM PLACE TO PLACE

My father, Henry Alexander de Thouars, after his retirement from the Amsterdam Trade Company, relocated to the city of Bandung in West Java. He accepted a position as bookkeeper with the Italian Mafalda Company, a chocolate and candy manufacturer. He worked for the Amsterdam Trade Company for twenty–five years and performed his duties as a chemical engineer. The change from chemical engineer with employees under him to a bookkeeper with people above him was a total turn around in job placement. It was a brand new office environment for my father.

Here in Bandung my Uncle Eddy de Vries, an awesome Pentjac Silat and Kun Tao expert, was living just several blocks away from where we had moved into a home my father rented for us. The home's owner, a certain Mr. Mar Chin, was a well–known Hokien Kun Tao master.

Bandung was, at that time, a wonderful place. In 1949, I went to school there as well. My experience of learning from my Uncle Eddy was truly one of the best moments of my life. Uncle Eddy was well built and full of muscle. He weighed around 280 pounds and stood 6'7" tall. He looked so big to me. He was a retired Colonial soldier. He had fought the Japanese and most of his combat duty involved fighting Ace in Sumatra during the last of the Ace revolts against the Dutch during the early 1900's.

I received constant training from my uncle after school. He trained me in the Nandang Serak Silat art. This form of Serak was taught directly under Pak Serak who gave instruction in Cheribon, the city where he was born. A few individuals like Edgar van der Groen, the Sultan of Pontianak, and Hamid III, General Berenschot, my Uncle Eddy, Groenewald and a few others were instructed in the art. Those individuals went straight to Cheribon and received training from Pak Serak. The Serak he taught was totally different from what Mas Djoet or Ma Roen was teaching.

To me, Serak Nandang was more practical and not as complex in practice as the Mas Djoet and Ma Roen methods. Through the guidance of Uncle Eddy, Edgar van der Grown and Groenwald, it was easier for us to comprehend when it comes to making the art more applicable. With a lot of influence of Ci Mande in the side stepping and moving in at the same time, it made the art simple and a more desirable learning experience for me. Like Kun Tao, the hand pattern was fluent and the quick and striking or low kicking at the places where an opponent was weakest in balance of his senses. This side of Serak is practiced as a dance form or Kembang.

My father was unhappy as a bookkeeper and accepted a job for another Dutch corporation. He was hired as a chemical engineer and we moved to East Java. It was here on the sugar cane factory of Pradjikan where my younger brother, Victor, and I were living with my parents. The corporation assigned my father a staff of employees for his home.

It was heaven for us to be able to live more freely than in any city. I got acquainted with East Javanese Silat here. I was able to witness first hand a fight between a tiny, thin gardener and a heavy set Dutchman, who had hired the small Indonesian native.

The physical disturbance between the two men started when the Dutchman was unfairly accusing his employee of stealing something from his provision room. Mr. Jokum, the Dutchman, was under my father and his house was located right beside ours. His mistake was accusing the little Indonesian gardener for something he had misplaced. When the Dutchman wanted to fire the little employee on the spot, the native Indonesian refused to leave and became incensed with anger. The natives from the region of East Java where the factory was located, near the cities of Situbondo and Bondowoso, were considered as half breeds. They were honest and good people. When their honor was at stake, they became hard to reckon with.

It was a moment of total frustration for the Dutchman. Unable to move his little employee, he grabbed a broomstick out of anguish. He swung with all his might at the gardener. He had just made another big mistake. Every time he tried to land the stick forcefully on the native's body, the little native easily ditched or leaped over the broomstick, than landed a kick against the Dutchman's groin or gave him an open palm slap on the head. After several attempts of swinging his stick around, his intent ended in a fruitless try. The little gardener had a satisfying smile and answered every attack with a reprisal of his counter. Each and every attempt the Dutchman made was directly answered with a kick against his "marital equipment" and immediately followed up with merciless and brutal open palm blows to the face of his bigger opponent.

The fight only lasted, maybe, ten minutes. Suddenly Mr. Jokum held both his hands over his lower body parts and literally sunk to the ground full of agony. Shielded from Mr. Jokum was a small blade that had been hidden in the gardener's sarong. The gardener stood looking down at his boss. He was not about to use the knife on him. He actually liked the Dutchman as a man. When the Dutchman wanted to slowly stand out of his position, his gardener held the little piece of steel gently on the Dutchman's throat and waited for the next action that followed. Mr. Jokum gently threw his arms up and, in disbelief, slowly came out of his position on the ground and stumbled into the house. He found out that it is never easy to hit a moving target.

I found out a few days later that the gardener's name was Murah (Cheap). He looked at me while standing at a corner in the Dutchman's front yard deciding if he was going to mow the grass or not. When we were eating breakfast one morning, my father mentioned that we could sue a gardener to take care of our yard. I said right away, "Dad, I have one for you. He's up for hire." My father asked, "is that the one that was kicking our neighbor's behind a day ago?" My head tilted up and down for approval and my dad told me to ask Murah to come and see him. But he first talked with his neighbor about his employee that my dad wanted to hire. Our neighbor was joyful and amazingly happy to lose his employee to us – the little Indonesian native he feared and respected.

Our houseman was a little scared after he saw Murah being hired as our yardman. He was showing us how great his Silat skills were and had no idea that Murah was the real deal. After a few days, I watched Murah work and understood why he was so strong, agile and able to leap the way he did. Our newly hired gardener was able to mow the grass with his parang, a long cutting blade. He used it like it was nothing and moved around on his knees or in a very low position. Once in a while, I saw Murah leap up and hold a snake in his hand that he caught before the reptile was able to bite him.

Murah always had a smile on his face and really enjoyed working on his knees. He was so fast cutting our two acres of grass field since he was so low to the ground. Our yard began to look like the yard of a Sultan's palace. I never saw our yard so clean and the trees neatly trimmed. We had eight papaya trees, a bunch of rose bushes and a coffee tree in our yard. There were also several banana and mango trees. We enjoyed refreshing our stomachs every day with fresh fruit.

Habitually, I liked the sketch the individuals who inspired me with my martial arts as I profoundly admired my teachers and the individuals that came in my focus. Murah certainly always stood out in praise with my grandest admiration for how he was and with his precise martial arts skills. It is therefore most appropriate that I like to add his facial expression in my illustration.

Before Murah came to work for my father, our grass and weeds were a couple of feet high. Wild animals could easily hide unnoticed and stalk us out of the bushy greens. Staff employees homes were located a distance of any of the nearby cities. The more I got to know the little gardener, the more of a liking I had for the new hire. He was incredibly full of energy and could pull weeds the whole day or mow the grass. He kept all three acres as clean as a whistle. My immense interest was in Murah's Pentjac Silat skills. They increased my curiosity and I wanted to learn his art. I had never witnessed such a "crafty" display of real martial arts by a small and tiny man against a much bigger opponent who had the skills to make minced mean out of him had he not been so skilled.

Finally, I had the courage to ask Murah if I could become his student. He told me flat out that he was not qualified enough to each Pentjac Silat Tjankring to me. I had to go to his teacher, Pak Ta Ing, who lived just a few kilometers away in a village. Guru Ta Ing was a very tiny man with a thin mustache and weighed not more than 120 pounds. Not to my surprise, he was the man my mother purchased her fresh meat and dairy products from. He had a small butcher shop not far from us.

After many journeys to the butcher shop to pick up my mother's orders, I finally got strongly encouraged, as Murah told me to do, by engaging myself in pleasant conversations with the little grey haired Indonesian man. I was truly amazed to find out that he little butcher had so much knowledge about the political struggle in the world concerning the Dutch and their presence in the Indonesian archipelago. The Guru could speak fluent Dutch which he had learned many years ago in a Dutch school for native Indonesians. He also served in the Colonial Army as a native soldier and fought against the Ace warriors in 1911. He was very loyal in his belief for the Dutch Queen Wilhelmina that he had served as a young teenager. He finished high school as a self taught student. He read lots of books and took private lessons from school teachers whenever he could.

Our conversations became more interesting each time. And each time, my mother scolded me from coming home late with the groceries. What really made me admire the old man was his knowledge and that he was always teaching me something. He liked the old administrator, a certain Mr. Bijten, who had already left for Holland after his retirement. I was again amazed when Ta Ing told me that he had trained Mr. Bijten in Pentjac Silat Tjangkring when he was still in charge of the factory. It was quite some time ago when the told me the experience he had had with the old administrator.

An administrator was put in charge of a sugar cane factory or any other plantation as a managing director over all staff employees and field workers.

I still smile when I think back to Mr. Bijten, a strong and tough minded Dutchman and well respected boss. He was highly thought of as a man in the upper class level of the corporate standings. He was practicing Silat and trained by the tiny butcher. The old administrator and the Silat guru were good friends. When I was in Holland, I visited the retired administrator and brought him a letter from our mutual guru. It must have shocked him, seeing a stranger on his front porch with a letter in hand to forward to him. He lived in the city of The Hague and it was more like a summer home on the beach.

After I gave him the letter and told him who I was, his stand off-ish attitude became more a fatherly friendliness. He took me inside the home where I met his wife, a friendly and just nice lady. I had to answer so many questions and he finally ended up teaching me his version of Tjangkring Silat that Ta Ing taught him. It's one thing to see, someone practicing Silat telling a lot of stories. It's another to see a huge man doing Silat with a kitchen knife, which was scarier than being plagued by a satanic demon.

I asked Guru about Tjangkring Silat and again the old Indonesian butcher lectured me on Silat and the history of Silat. It became a real education for me. It was worth listening to, coming from the mouth of an educator. It is a most profound reason that I was more informed than some other Silat experts who actually had more interest in only their styles. I had reasoned and logically debated many issues out of a historical point of view, rather than basing an essence by assuming the truth like so many people do when they lack sound information.

Just to see the old Guru, well in his seventies then, as he managed his blades in butchering meat using only simple kitchen knives was amazing. Even at his age and being so small and this, he could work for many hours without getting tired. He could slice a whole cow in three hours with just a long blade and a couple of boning knives. Each blade was carefully sharpened to a razor's edge, beyond the sharp edges of a Gillette set. Seeing the butcher at work taught me more that

I could ever have bargained for from a man who was going to teach me his art.

Finally, after many negotiations between the old Guru and myself, a worthless youngster who still had so much to learn, Guru Ta Ing allowed me to come and study with him. My teacher convinced my mother that Silat was good for me. It would teach me to defend myself. In exchange for the valuable lessons I received, I promised to help him by working in his shop. The place we lived was dangerous with blade oriented natives.

When I started my first lesson in Tjangkring, Guru taught me how to efficiently handle blades and knives and how to precisely cut anatomical regions of living species. In handling a blade, the object is to slice first, then cut and penetrate deep with a loose grip and angular motions while maintaining intense focus. The practice is consistent and you strive toward timing and accurate placement of the point of the blade to a point of impact by thrusting and slicing and moving the blade with angular motions to the body. You also cork screw a blade, knife or any pointed object deep through bone and flesh.

We trained our fingers in Kun Tao to penetrate flesh and bone with an energetic force. Two fingers are extended strongly in the twin dragon stroke. The low ground fighting style gave a practitioner of the art an advantage of making use of the volcanic terrain. You are able to move around instinctively to counter, sweep, trap, and ditch and use springy legs to kick or hold a knife between the toes.

This art's history goes back to the mid–1800's and was founded by Tomo, a man and trader who lived on the Island of Madura for a long time. The man trained and fought with warrior tribesmen who were inhabitants of Sumbawa, Maccassar, Celebes and other islands. Through his intense battles, he developed a fierce reputation. He finally settled on Java's east coast. It was here in Situbondo when Ta Ing met Tomo. He received many years of instruction under Tomo and ended up being his disciple. Ta Ing was largely responsible for having taught the art in the Bondowoso region of East Java.

To an extent, I prefer East Javanese Silat over the Sunda Silat when blades are involved. The Javanese Silat systems of East Java draw their influence back to the Sultanate's time period of the Mataram Empire. Since that time in the ninth century, the combative systems never focused on structured practice and instead were more combat oriented without a standardized method of training.

Tjangkring Silat was referred to as the Art of Glistening Blades because of the sparkle of the blade under the sun. The sparkle of steel and the reflection of the sun was often confusing for an opponent during battle. The Tjangkring player was completely comprehensive in his blade training and often lured opponents in becoming blinded by the glare of the sparkling reflection of his blade.

Training in Pencak in East Java is very hard as is consists mostly of low posture training and maintains a schedule of high leaps, then coming down like a monkey to the ground and punching rocks. Historically since the Sultanate of Mataram was created as a Hindu and Buddhist empire, it was perhaps originated by a Mongol warrior in the nature of aggressiveness in fighting. The warriors at the time were only trained for direct combat and, as a result, any structured system would be a set back. There are no rules or physical structure to train the fighters in combat. The unstructured systems are more agile and a more natural expression for offense or defense. The high leaps are merely designed to jump and land on an opponent – to slice an opponent's throat or open a possibility to attack and strike against an adversary's most vulnerable position.

Someone highly trained in this East Javanese combative system is unpredictably agile and exchanges a moment of grace into a combative art of lightening speed and extreme fury. What was considered in the art as jurus we had to practice related more to a free flow with unorganized hand motions. It was like countering your own attack against yourself and fighting your own shadow. The training method was called mirror hands or Katja.

In the beginning when I started to train, blocking yourself through a mirror image of yourself was the hardest part of practice and almost impossible to do. As time evolved, I had gotten into blade confrontations with others and was glad for the training my teacher provided to me. The lessons learned paid off in the long run. In my later years, that simple practice saved my life many times. I will always treasure and appreciate the Guru's instructions, especially with a knife or blade.

How does one describe the practice of anything. Nothing is an accurate description of how it feels to be in a sport for a number of years and how it relates to the practice of martial arts. A question came to mind many times: what did one achieve as an educated guess and how can it be remembered over the years? To simply answer the question in one sentence, it is the painstaking events that are most remembered that the actual practice regarding the fighting arts.

After more than sixty years of learning, training and living the practice as a way of life, one comes to find out that everything has to come to an end, only to start all over again. The circle of life continues. The way I see life most clearly is like a mirror within and captured in a frame.

In my years of practice and study of martial arts, I found simplicity in nothing than just training with an empty mind and soul. The more the mind frees itself from desires, stress or concentration, the more the body becomes free in physical action and gains healthy energy.

It is always the physical essence that grows old while the spirit remains untouched. The word "nothing" has played an important part of my psychological reasoning when dealing with people. The word is an essence of my thinking and helped me overcome a stressful obstacle. I just removed it as a hustle that would otherwise become a monkey on my back.

The best thing in life that I ever did was ignoring the spit balls that were thrown at me. Even my blood family, like brothers or sisters, are remarkably an avoidance if it is at all possible through philosophical logic. My own brothers once accused me for not ever having practiced martial arts in my life. How cute! Furthermore, I was spoken of for never having had any interest in martial arts and lacked the physical abilities for understanding movements. Seriously now? How funny for someone not knowing anything about martial arts to know how to write on many subjects through comprehension.

An older brother told me to use the name Ratu Duri Silat for my martial arts. Ratu means foreign. Duri is similar to a thorn. Silat has all ready been explained. To keep the peace, I used that name for a short while and later changed it to Kun Tao Silat de Thouars.

My younger brother thought I needed to learn more about how to structure my system into a standardized martial art. He even came to my hotel room to tell me that. I have already practiced my system for sixty years. Two other individuals I once trained thought of taking over my soul and caused a lot of trouble in the internet gossip column. My family was harassed. Later on they thought they could play a foolish horse with the government and tried to sue the Vice President of the United States, the governor of Colorado and several law enforcement agencies, while trying to represent themselves in court. At the end they ended up running into a huge wall, as a reward of course!

I am all for healthy laughter when it comes to dealing with the human race. I often thought to myself how can people be so intelligent and also so stupid? If intelligence is used the wrong way, then common sense needs to be studied by those people.

In the next pages, I will draw some illustrations concerning the Guru Pak Ta Ing, the opening set of Kun Tao Silat de Thouars, a Northern Shantung set and a from of Tjangkring Silat.

Pak Sa-ing in his 70's

Opening set of kun tao silat de thouars. The set is northern shan-tung kun tao from its origin. This set is a very important set and is used as an opening for almost any of our forms – and by closing.

Hopefully with the conclusion of Part 12, I have done some justice to my Kun Tao and Silat teachers and how the history of events relates to the current martial arts endeavors. The most laughable moments in my life I have experienced came through the mouths of some considered to be martial arts masters. They said everything looks the same. For the masses, there are masters of martial arts. From my point of view, everyone considering himself a master has not reached the level of maturity in thinking. People who claimed that saying in statements were truly excellent practitioners in just what they were doing. If one considers himself a master, he will have to know all the martial arts. The truth in the nature of the answer lies in God's hands. He is the one who knows!

In evaluating the words of what was said to me, it is to their misfortune and their greater lack of comprehension that no fighting art can ever be the same. No Silat art can be a Silat art and no Kun Tao art can be a Kun Tao art as one art because there is an incredible difference in each system and how they were originally formatted by the founders.

The martial arts and their secrets relate to only one idea of thinking – what it pertains to and how the flavor has been received through the endeavor of practice. To take ones art and constructively adding a flamboyancy of philosophy in the thought process of students by educating them that their school was founded upon one perfect man's idea. Take the fist arts for instance where it leads to and stumble on the side of a huge retaining wall in front of us. The wall carries many names, most are familiar to us. Take into consideration the word Kempo or Kenpo. Chuan Fa, Shuan Shu, Kun Tao, Kuen Tao, Kun Taw, Kung Fu, and Gung Fu all relate to a meaningful and dialectic expression for who is saying it. The way Chinese Kempo or Japanese Kenpo is practiced is a total opposite of my own Kun Tao training in Indonesia.

West Javanese Silat and East Javanese Silat are totally different in philosophy, psychology and the practice of a methodology in training. There has to be and it's how it should be. Otherwise, we have nothing that can be compared to anything and everything. Through my illustrations, I hope to present the reader in the next chapters a variety of approaches as how one art differs from another.

It is spiritually and humanly impossible to put all Hakka Kun Tao styles under one category. There are many Hakka people practicing one thing or another and in what they have trained pertains to old Shao Lin boxing. It would be respectfully referred to as old Fu Jaws or old hand Kung Fu practitioners. There are many Hakka people and each family had a different style of martial practice. I will cover more on the Hakka people in a special chapter and also with some drawings concerning the combative arts in my own practice.

The energy in which Hakka as a form of combat training and in fighting is perceived only through the practice of Hakka Kun Tao as a class on its own. There are some great individuals, also highly ranked and very good in martial arts practices who have known me for many years, have tried to duplicate my ways or the movements of my most well trained practitioners came to a stop and were lost and running out of ideas for material to teach. They called the things they had taken out my system and called it their teacher's art. The only problem those individuals are faced with is to keep on forgetting that anywhere and everywhere there are a few of my good practitioners around who know the art like an open dictionary.

Another laughter for my sharing with those that read my book, the masters who took from me and are known to express themselves by criticizing me to an extreme, keep on forgetting that what we are doing does not fill up an empty bucket, unless it is water. Actually, I am deeply honored that those masters who took from me because imitation in any form is the best recognition.

After having trained in the practice of Hakka Kun Tao for most of my life, my main interests remain in Hakka with its traditions, customs and culture. I have closed my doors to outsiders and even old acquaintances. In what I had experienced was my best schooling on Earth. I respect all martial arts practices and individuals who are comprehensive of understanding as mature people. To them my house is always wide open. To the ones that don't understand me, they are just a hindrance to my soul and a waste of time. They preclude an expansion of any friendly relationship with others.

PART 13
HISTORY AND THE ARTS

Taking our past and present into account, the focus of my attention was fully geared to exploring resourcefully the start of martial arts expansion throughout the world. A world that has become smaller to travel. Quite often, there were discussions relating to any form of martial practice. A myriad of which many of the reasoning from martial arts experts has gone through constant changes. Mankind has undergone through significant times in history. Every since the caveman, from fire building to the shaping of tools, there was a practice for survival and self defense, with or without weapons. The nature of man is aggressive and defensive.

As civilization began to grow like a weed in mankind's world and a society controlled by laws, arts of combat were turned into social sports where the best grappler, best pugilist or best stone thrower was more interesting to man. From the beginning when man was still unorganized and dissocial, prior to the invention of governments, man was a culture builder and was forced to create a police force to uphold social law structure.

Over thousands of years, man organized fleets and armies and started to conquer lands and territories for their own habitat. In ancient times, centuries before Christ, states were formed from city states. Later countries erected a social environment and ended up becoming countries and nations. When countries came into existence, leaders came out of nations.

In 320 BC, King Phillip of Macedonia, father of Alexander the Great, widely improved city states in politics and created well trained armies. The Kings of Syria and Babylonia were constantly attacking the State of Greece. They failed at times because King Phillip's army had better field commanders and trained soldiers. When King Phillip was assassinated in 326 BC Alexander the Great, who at 26, assumed control over his father's army.

After Alexander took control over the Macedonians, he immediately began his conquest to invade neighboring countries. He felt that with expansion and conquering more countries, he would secure Macedonia and Greece or more territory and progress. The greatest battle he fought was against the Persian King. Persia, at the time, was the largest empire and controlled nations like Syria, Iraq, Saudi

Arabia, Jordan, Babylon, Turkey, Egypt and the eastern shores of India. As a young leader, Alexander and his smaller army had to face the Persians who came in great force with 250,000 men. Alexander had only 25,000 under his command. The Persians outnumbered the Macedonians ten to one.

The Persians had Alexander and his army surrounded and far greater force in manpower. With the mindset of a genius, Alexander designed a counter strategy to let his army attack the center of their strong formation. This military counter attack made Alexander the Great one of the world's greatest field commanders. By breaking through the Persian defense, Alexander was able to defeat the Persian king's largest army. The Persian king was, at that time, considered to be the King of Kings. Darius III was overthrown by the Macedonian king and Alexander seized a huge territory including Anatolia, Syria, Phoenicia, Judea, Gaza, Egypt, Bactria, and Mesopotamia.

My failure in life is that I live through history and recall almost every battle. Through my imagination, I visualize myself back in time. Every one of those events relate to give our martial arts a place of inheritance in history. One example is that boxing was introduced in Egypt by Alexander the Great when he overthrew the Persians. Boxing gloves were invented in Sparta and later used in the Greek and Roman Olympics. Without mentioning the history, I would not be able to evaluate myself and my martial arts and how they relate to all the fighting arts in the world from historical events.

Prior to his death, Alexander had planned to extend his Macedonian Empire to Carthage, Rome and the Iberian Peninsula for military and merchant expansion. Unfortunately at a young age, Alexander the Great died in Babylon. According to one of the Esagila Temple recordings, Alexander died on the evening of June 11th in 323 BC. Sadly, according to man's nature, King Phillip was assassinated by one of his own officers, the Captain of his Bodyguard, Pausanias). Time and space can never justify Alexander the Great to the fullest. It is the reason I only collectively took some of the highlights of this magnificent genius and his place in history.

The true start of the Olympics began in Greece during the years before Christ and were later adopted by the Romans under Julius Caesar in 46 BC. Caesar also introduced the Julian calendar, which divided each year into twelve months. Time, week, month and hours in each calendar year is important for medical observation. In every period the days, hours, minutes and seconds play an important part in our healing process.

Organized combat sprang forth throughout history, from trained soldiers to individual combatants. Through improvement in resources of information, the matter in which martial arts became scientific studies in physical strength and health.

A VIEW ON CHINESE KUN TAO

China, through thousands of years of evolution left behind traces of China's involvement in cultural influences in countries and nations of the world. Interestingly through the discoveries of my study of history, I found that China as an ancient civilization and highly cultured nation was strongly bound and focused in a background of culture and tradition. It was flourishing and managed to survive while other civilizations like Egypt, Babylon and Assyria faded away. Incredibly, China as a nation influenced with such magnitude that has never been surpassed by other cultures. Its presence in the boundaries of other nations who inhabited the lands of Asia and the Malay Peninsula left behind a heredity of trade, fine arts, batik (cloth weaving) and customs and traditions. This was thousands of years before Christ.

Chinese martial arts was consistently improving during China's conquest to annex other countries. Through thousands of years in battle and in conflicts, Chinese armies became superbly trained and experienced in military warfare (Wu Shu). Combative systems were considered in the 25th century BC as military arts of war by the generals who themselves were involved in each battle and created fighting arts of their own. From the beginning when the founder of the Chinese nation, the Emperor Fu, had ruled China thousands of years ago, the emperor creating fighting methods for his armies to practice. He also invented the healing arts of Gi Gung, a refined art in which abdominal breathing exercises can achieve a higher level of health. The healing arts and fighting arts are one in the same.

To the Chinese, the word Kun Tao relates to nothing. It is meaningless and the word simply does not exist. The Mandarin Chinese considered themselves the only pure race of higher class standing over other Chinese. An exact expression for the word Kun Tao comes only in the Hokien dialect as fist art. People of Hokien are today still looked upon as foreigners. The word Hokien means foreign. People out of Fuek Chin are better accepted and are referred to as skilled laborers or carpenters.

It was during an era of Yuan Shih– K'ai (1859–1916) that Yuan as a commander of the armies of the North Zone added the long spear hand technique of Kun Tao to the Wu Shu practiced in armies under him. Yuan, during his time, executed many of the scholars and educators. An unfavorable reaction by conservative circles in government, he abandoned the scholars and reformers. During that time, K'ang Yu–Wei and his disciple Liang Chi'I–Chi,Ao (1873–1920) were two boxers from the North that escaped to Japan. They formed an association to protect the Emperor. They introduced some of their fighting techniques to some Japanese masters that in later years belonged to the Black Dragon Society.

The long hand technique in Wu Kung Kun Tao and all of the Hakka system was influenced by the spear and sword fighting methods of the North. Through constant practice in training of fast piercing and thrusting techniques out of very low horse stance positions became very important to understanding the launching art. When lashing out at an opponent through the constant conflict, a well practiced fighter in Wu Kung Kun Tao can actually penetrate through the skin and muscle with a spear hand technique (twin dragon) to reach the internal organs of his adversary. Everything practiced in Kun Tao is based on constant and intensive training of self discipline, motion, empty space, awareness of surrounding, and the use of explosive actions with the intent of appropriate timing on the blood stream of an opponent. The Wu sets are a form of the North and the Kung of the South.

Hopefully through my illustrations of Hakka Kun Tao and the Indonesian arts most familiar to me I can justify my writing on the subject. The history added to my manuscript was necessary for me to relate in my writing how history and survival have existed since Adam and Eve. It was all for the good of mankind to improve ways of combat through historical events. No martial arts can remain the same. Of all the arts I was introduced to, I found the Pentjac Silat Tjangkring a very difficult art to learn, unless one is born into the culture. My health improved only by the practice of the art.

HA KA KUN TAO

The Long Fist or Spear Hand technique was designed for practice by Yan Shih K'ai, a general (martial arts leader) of the North from his experience during combat. Once when the general was cut off from his troops in Kwan Tung, he had to ward off several wild tribesmen on horses. As the horsemen came charging in to him, the general moved swiftly through the encirclement and broke the formation of his adversaries. During the course of his action in defense of himself, Yan with the agility and precision of his long spear, was able to pierce through the bodies of some opponents and at the same time chopped their heads off. The general was so quick with his piercing and slashing techniques that he left his startled adversaries behind when he escaped the attack. This is a reproduction of Yah Shih K'ai's photo, taken from a history book. This is a pencil drawing by the author. Yan Shih K'ai (1859–1916)

214.

PRELUDING A RESOURCEFUL TRUTH

After resourceful studies concerning martial arts, in particular some of the arts practiced here in the United States, great performers of the Indonesian fighting arts of Pentjac Silat came many years ago to this country of milk and honey and taught their arts. The arts they were teaching were excellent and absolutely commendable. Many came to study their secretive styles. After setting foot on this great country's ground, they began overloading themselves with absolutely magnificent titles such as Pendekar, Ma Ha Guru, Great Grandmaster, Supreme Grandmaster, Professor, and Guru Besar and made their loyal followers subject to their demands. They had to secure a throne to sit on. At this point there is no prelude to turn back and return back to Earth or a simple life structure.

Being in the martial arts for many decades, throughout my teaching career and after retirement, I evaluated my own path to glory. It was a resourceful study by reading history books and studying events concerning medieval combat, the military art of war and collectively gathered information on those specific fighting arts of the Indonesian Pentjac Silat styles.

The supreme grandmasters I was relating to were, up to a point, sharing misleading information with their students who were all ears, listening to confusing stories and history about the art they were learning. The teacher I referred to made a supremely grand mistake by sharing information that was told by family at home, mainly uncles and aunties. They were fool hearted explaining how the founder of their specific style had studied five Chinese systems, four Indian arts, and more Indonesian combative arts. I was overwhelmed in my search for the truth since I was present and had also listened to those stories at home long ago. They were consistently highly controversial explanations of their version of the truth.

In knowing how meticulous American students are by nature and how regimented they are in thinking, they hung on almost every word and sentence in their notebooks. As time moved on and the Pentjac Silat arts found potential growth throughout the United States, the Supreme Grandmasters started to change the history in their imagination and later claimed to the same students that they art they were studying had no Chinese influences.

To satisfy my curiosity and wanting to make sure students were receiving correct information, I found out that the background of their combative arts they were teaching were actually Chinese martial arts practices. Since the beginning, I had known the truth, just by observing the art that was taught and practiced by these supreme Grandmasters. The art drew its roots back to the basic fundamentals of I Shing Yie when it comes to the art of hitting and the movements of Tai Chi Chuan (the grand ultimate fist) and some basic Kung Fu. The information I received was that the supreme Grandmasters were originally taught an incomplete version of the Chinese art. They lacked the internal side in their practice of the art. The line system in which they based their advances was taken out of the basic format of line practice of fencing books and not out of schools that taught Olympic or fencing styles for self defense.

In my closing statements concerning the Indonesian fighting arts, the true facts of history can only be found in the sources out of Indonesia. Anywhere else can only be described as secondary information. The supreme Grandmasters taught their art with highly rated commendation and with my respect. In a true sense, the art they practice suits the nature of the Dutch to its fullest justice, rather than how it occurred in Indonesia where the art came from.

A SHAMEFUL TRUTH

As was claimed by some excellent Kempo practitioners, they were indeed so well seasoned in their arts that there can never be any justification for their denial of their lasting presence at the expense of their own contradictory statements. They could protect their intent for reinventing my system and tell the world that they knew forty of my forms I never taught them. Everything I do looks the same in a Kempo structure.

Since the manuscript has come near to completion, I wish to clarify those statements by clearly illustrating the difference in technique, movements and approaches in combat through my drawings in this book. One art is not the same and any form or juru has to be done in the same way in practice and training each and every time. By changing an art form or system and adding in what one likes for himself without crediting others, like some greats in the martial arts world, they just reinvent the wheel in Kempo mentality. The same individuals who issued those statements saw me first and took from me what they needed to flavor their system. They later criticized me for everything concerning my practice. Amen for the due process of time. I wish them the very best for being the Guru first and later, as time slips away, for being considered a horse's ass. From my part, the more spit balls are thrown at me, the more I practice my art. One of my Kung Fu brothers once told me, "Willem, don't worry. Always understand that imitation is the best form of flattery." A true statement!

In the next pages, I constructively illustrate and draw the complexity in combat between styles of a short spear long hand set of Hakka Kun Tao. This particular Kun Tao style pertains to the movements of the fire dragon. All the drawings are made simple and are self explanatory for the non complexity of understanding.

YanSung kun tao

East Javanese Style

Fan Lung Kun tao
(spearhand set)

1

2

3

4

PART 14

PHILOSOPHY AND INTERNAL KUN TAO

Philosophy as a subject of consideration is the greatest base for a focus of mental expansion. It helps the mind to be productive and brings a deeper sense of understanding. Even in a fraction of a second when my mind is at work, I can perceive for just that instant that the mind is already philosophically inclined with reality in theory. It is also experiencing a change in sensitivity of impulse in human nature.

My strongest point in all studies, if I had to make a choice, would always be the rebirth of philosophy for my own conscious belief. It also made a total difference for me as a martial arts practitioner in discovering the true sense for practicing the fighting arts and how they relate to history and to the healing arts by exploring facts and function. Without any common sense in good gesture in training, trying to achieve excellence would be a failure. There can never be a strong physical practice in any combative art without the presence of internal health.

History is truly the very best learning tool. A journey to our past in which we can actually touch, philosophically, our heritage and expand our search for the truth in what is real and what is fiction. As my martial arts journey comes to an end, my other journey starts to expand more comprehensively of traveling to a zone in which I like to reach a "plateau" of better self understanding.

In what my teachers taught me in the practice of Kun Tao and Pencak Silat will always remain a fact of my life. The purity of physical torture and mental understanding and internal health and martial training are one in the same. It was a main source of comprehensively enhancing my journey in physical training and clearly shapes a picture in my mind of bettering myself in a philosophical sense. Who needs diplomas even for decorating a living room wall? If it pertains to a job qualification, it would be very helpful to find a means of learning a living. Martial arts in the world we live in pertains only to entertainment and not a program that is even designed to improve health. Lots of diplomas and certifications I received in my lifetime which were given to me by most distinguished masters of martial arts practices were given in recognition of my martial arts achievements. I am thankful, of course, for the thought alone, but I lost them all in trash cans where they accidentally went while moving from house to house. I kept some that I was able to survive my ordeals. What was taught to me is what I have preached my entire life. Diplomas and wall papers can never compete with eternal knowledge.

History is an excellent learning tool to see there is always so much to learn from even the greatest of geniuses. Consider their failure to one's own success in a far lesser margin. It would be shamefully thought of if one considered himself in greatness to Napoleon Bonaparte, who fought more battles than even Alexander the Great, but could learn from Napoleon's creation of social successes and established a habit for a good listener. The Emperor could write a letter and listen to ten advisors at the same time. His greatest failure was his greed and ego. This can be helpful in comparing oneself with the social struggle of anyone else and the lust for recognition to be the best over others. This can relate to most masters who are actually not deserving to be masters. From my experience, it is always better to leave one's ego at home where it belongs.

Here are a few words of wisdom that I would like to share with the reader. These are the reasons for my successful life at home and in friendship with many.

Always think simple and stay simple.

Always strive to be better and allow yourself to make mistakes.

Don't get bent out of shape. If you do, realize that mistakes are actually not mistakes. There is something on tomorrow's horizon.

When you train, just do it and nothing else.

Don't look for perfection. It does not exist.

Be practical and think practical.

Be healthy and think healthy.

When you play games, think of them as games.

Only professionals can think seriously about the games they are playing.

Look at life for what it is worth and always relax. Hopefully you will see tomorrow's sunshine.

Sometimes when things are not going well in trying to achieve beyond one's intent for greater expectations, there is a failure of a tool of understanding to strive better. The moments of joy can turn into a sad experience. When one is successful in one thing, forget and don't dwell on it any longer. What was a success yesterday is a total chance the next day. Each tunnel has an end. Discovering with one's own vision means that there is something beyond the horizon. Negative and strong positive impulses are actually the creation for sharp reasoning.

THE TAO

The way of the Tao, or the natural way of the universe, is a way in which nature moves the elements and all life forces of heaven and Earth together as one principle. The universe relates to all life forces in existence; above in the stars and in heaven and hell. To humans, hell is here on Earth. It minimizes feelings or compassions and only does one thing very well. As a life force, it destroys and rebuilds.

Physical combat is the very best energy one can produce for an intent for self–defense, a pleasurable engagement or just for the sake of fighting. The art of self defense is a basic understanding of evading, deflecting, ditching and with a prompt response of countering any oncoming brute force with the best energy from within. The thought process in martial behavior is caused through training of practicing shadow boxing or theory in fighting. Only after the thinking starts to take over, the body begins to slack off and lose energy.

In Hakka Tun Kao, the art of primitivism in the actualization of combat was always shadowed by the history of the Hakka nomadic tribal warriors of the past. They fought on horses during armed or unarmed conflicts. They also won many battle engagements. They were known as the most aggressive warrior nomadic tribesmen. Retreat in any conflict was never an option for these horsemen of Mongolia. During combat, the Hakka fighters were taking in and delivering more physical punishment without and without exhaustion maintained their highly coordinated attacks and high energy. Adversaries that were involved in combating the Hakka warriors found them fearsome and unstoppable. They were constantly on the attack with their brutal skills and fighting skills.

Therefore in practice, the Hakka Kun Tao forms have to be done with energy and speed. Energy and speed are two important principalities in most of the Hakka Kun Tao systems. The way a practitioner in Kun Tao moves or practices his art is also the same way he battles.

Considering the efforts in training in Kun Tao will have a great and beneficial result in the end – in growing older and staying energetic. Correct positioning and lining up the skeletal figure and shoulders in coordination with footwork in a very low deep horse stance, the body as a whole is constantly moving without the head changing position. The neck remains straight and in place. Low horse riding stances shorten the distance between an opponent and a Kun Tao practitioner. A low horse stance training method offers many valid options for covering distance quickly with leaps in the air or fast rolls on the ground.

The internal arts are of significant importance in training. It would be impossible to even train, practice, kick or punch correctly without appropriate breathing exercises. Stamina provides the best understanding of one's own body capabilities. Incorrect breathing stimulates a shortness of air intake and will cause someone to become breathless, ending with a stroke or violent heart attack. Internal breathing exercises of the lower abdominal region is, perhaps, the most important Gi Gung exercise to cultivate a bloodstream for accurate pumping of blood flow to the heart and oxidation to the brain cells.

The Nei Gung breathing exercises are designed to defensively prevent a physical injury to the internal organs of the body during combat. The mind, body and spirit become a human shield to ward off an oncoming brute force and deflect an attack to turn the same force toward an attacker. Lots of Iron Skin training is required to even understand the practice of Nei Gung as a defensive system. Breathing sounds are an opposite reaction to the Gi Gung breathing exercises for health. There are many different sound techniques to make a Gi Gung art most applicable.

Wei Kung as a subject of study is an opposite over the Gi Gung and Nei Gung. The intake of air is even more complex than the other two internal practices. In Wei Kung, everything is constructed for total offense and stamina is based on forwarding an energetic force with speed and agility to an opponent's internal nervous system. When the three principles of internal practice Gi Gung, Nei Gung and Wei Kung is used together as one force, it is an unstoppable force in action with deadly results.

In some of my drawings, I will illustrate the use of Du Mak points, either to heal or destroy the muscles, bone structure or internal organ of the body. A Dumak expert, after many years of training, will strike or attack the bloodstream with a soft touch. This will cause a timed delayed reaction in the bloodstream and can stop the heartbeat, lungs or brain cells from getting blood. Everything is done after careful and long intense study of a time table. A timetable is a chart that indicates the position of the moon that is an influencing factor for the month, week, and day and, specifically, an hour a technique is placed on a body with intent.

The bloodstream is constantly changing with the weather, environment and the position of the moon. An Iron Palm expert, through brute force, will destroy everything he touches after a long period of training. A vibrating palm expert will destroy things through soft sensitivity. He uses only a soft, vibrating touch that causes bone structure to collapse in certain places. Bone becomes cement or powder from the heat expansion caused by an open palm strike. With a correctly timed action, a finger Du Mak touch will trigger a delayed reaction in the blood flow and death will occur in hours or a few days after. Only another Du Mak expert can cure a Du Mak touch from an expert intent on slowly killing someone.

ANATOMICAL chart. and shitting charts.
Numbers are left out for reasons of my own.

182

FENCING, THE ART OF IMPORTANCE

In concluding my second book, I would like to add that I studied for a short time under one of Belgium's finest fencing experts. This is my tribute to the man and the short experience I had in his art of dualistic fencing.

Considering that most forms of combat are easy to relate to the fighting methods of armed engagements by armies of the past, it has improved all our skills of today's practices in combat. Years ago, I would have disagreed with anyone to call the knowledge of fighting styles a practice of martial arts. At the heart of realism, any practice of fighting came through a much greater source. It came through thousands of years of experiencing battle and was fought by armies around the globe in a physical struggle for survival.

When I first came to Europe and lived in Holland in the 1950s, I had the great fortune of meeting Jan Leville, a young Frenchman. He asked me if I did any sports. I told him what I did socially and in training. After listening to what he did as a student of a fencing master in Belgium, I became curious and excited to learn.

I found that that Jan practiced dualistic and Olympic style fencing and used the saber well enough to enter competition. He also knew the sword, foil, and short and long daggers. When he demonstrated on me his blade work and how fast, agile and quick he thrusted through my martial arts positions, I got a second opinion relating to my own bladed art practice. Much to my surprise, I also discovered that Jan was sometimes taught tricks by Fred Cavens, a friend of his sword master who taught Basil Rathbone, the famous British American actor, the art of fencing. I think that Rathbone was the very best Sherlock Holmes on the silver screen.

Several weeks after our meeting, Jan took me on a trip with him to Brussels, which is not far from Amsterdam, where I was living. We had an interesting trip through France, Belgium and Italy and we stayed away for weeks. It was a quite different experience, practicing with the small Indonesian natives and the much stronger Europeans. It was a reality check for me to discover something new with other people, in other countries and other languages. I also knew then that I wanted to learn fencing for the experience alone. It could help me overcome my "boxed in" mentality out of my own habitual practice. Mentally, I had to overcome so much of the dullness that was inhabiting a few other martial arts practitioners out of Indonesia (other Dutch Indonesians) who were set in their minds.

As a raw beginner and not knowing anything, I participated in most events and was amazed how much there was to learn about combat. Opposite of what I was used to, I think Kun Tao training was harsh on low horse stances and brutally unforgiving for the physical torture alone. The stamina and endurance for fencing is so much more eloquent, graceful and even more demanding than my previous training in the forest.

A daily endeavor in training to fence consists of a three kilometer run, jumping rope for a half hour, then boxing on a schedule of four rounds and the final hours of work with another line training on a very large diagram on the ground. I never came to learn ballet for agility because I was too short on time for my training. Preparing oneself for combat within the mental structure of the European mindset was very difficult to embrace after being so accustomed to a way of life in the Islands. After being beat up embarrassingly by better trained people who were indeed much stronger than myself, I was convinced that the two unequal poles, like the currents of a battery, can blend Eastern and Western culture well.

It was never my interest in the fighting aspects because I was never a fighter like most people. I only fought when I had to. I would rather fight myself out of a fight than get into one. To know myself better martially, I had to go through a lengthy process of immensely difficult training and become psychologically, philosophically, and strategically stronger. It is always for an interest in better health to feel better about one's own self than by going by the thought process of others.

The combat experience was interesting and stressful and took a lot out of me. At some point during practice, I had to puke and fell exhausted, unable to endure any more fighting with sticks, blades, and foils and needed to take a break. Realistic bombardments of sticks and other objects being blasted at you was so tiresome that lifting an arm became almost impossible with all the crushing, bashing and smashing each other for hours. I understood then that fighting for pleasure was really not my game, but the learning process to maturity was the most important endeavor of my trip.

What made me laugh was when Jan, during one of our recesses said that I was so unstructured and was like a cat in a bad top. Jan laughed, rolling over the grass field where we were taking a break, and said, "I've never seen a skinny guy like you fight so neurotically and successfully out of a fighting position." Most of the other guys felt uncomfortable fighting a very unstructured opponent. Every time they moved into me with precision, I encountered each attack from the side with my lack of experience in fencing. The attacks punctured the shielded body of my training partner and despite the blows and strikes, they landed on me. My whole body was purple and blue from the dots and sliced imprints left behind.

The time spent with Jan on tour will always be a treasure to me I will keep for the rest of my life. While my brothers, Maurice, Paul and Victor, were only training in Serak, I went through the practice of the art. It was more of a Dutch version for the strong upper body alignment and strong body leverage. They move in like bulls, while the Serak in Indonesia is more practiced out of a very low position and is more Kun Tao originated. There is nothing wrong with either practice. When one is large bodied, it makes more sense to do the Dutch way. When one is thin like me or small, I rather prefer the low version.

My teacher, Monsieur Le Grande, was a highly unorthodox oriented fighter with his beliefs in fencing. He handled foils or any weapon like chop sticks and moved the useful killing tools as if they were little bamboo sticks to deliver strikes or blows. Always loose on his grip, he would move fast with his fingertips to penetrate a body so quickly that no one noticed a thing.

This most amazing gentleman was quite a master of fencing crafts when I saw him fence one of his best disciples in the old school building. The man he squared off was strong and fast and the two men fought several rounds when at a moment of well timed attack, Monsieur's disciple launched in so fast that my eyes could hardly follow the action. During that instant, the master leaped backward over a stack of empty wooden crates and accurately placed a "Z" on the flannel shirt his fencing partner wore, without one scratch on his body. They were so good that they did not wear protective gear. I heard that only occasionally did someone sustain a small injury.

All forms of combat have to be equally respected even it it's not your own practice. When someone thinks too much of himself, he might be in for a surprise when he shows himself to be a lesser opponent in battle. The line training on the diagram is helpful for the understanding of angularity for moving and defending oneself with many possibilities, rather than a straight line attack. Take away all the weapons of an excellent dualistic fencer, one who is strongly organized, and one will run into an arsenal of strong energetic blocks, hard internal punches, hard hitting elbow strokes, unorthodox knee butts, leg traps, leg sweeps and some hard throws. A well trained and seasoned "all around" fencer does not need any other martial arts for his self defense. He already has his combant needs in his own practice.

I will close by adding some drawings of the body positioning of Kun Tao in relation to the physical placement of a fencer. Both aspects from my point of view are relatively the same and perhaps came at one time from the same school of practice long ago.

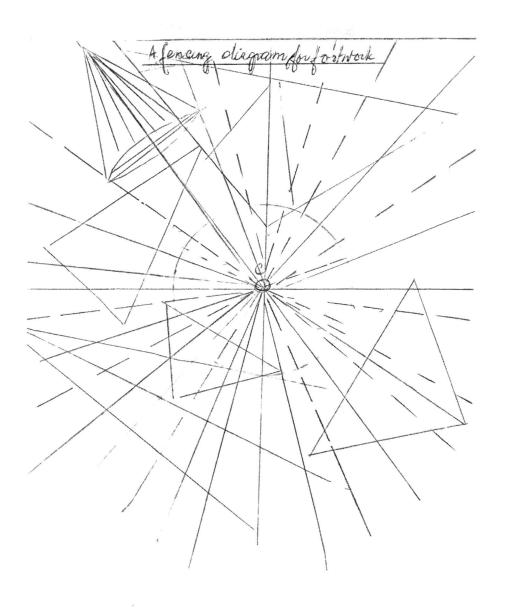

A fencing diagram for footwork

SouTHERN kun Too and in relation to position
of fencing stances.

1

2

3

4

kum tao stance

fencing stance

1

2

3

The musketeer's grip was created by the Musketeers, a loyal guard to the French king. The foil or sword was loosely held and with the flip of the thumb, a pointed weapons is driven clear through the human body. Even parrying or blocking was done with a loose grip. As the position indicates, this is a blocking or on guard position.

CONCLUSION

In closing my second book, I would like to express my feelings concerning the martial arts and their purpose. Over a period of 60 years. I have viewed the world of martial arts from Judo, Karate, Tae Kwon Do, Kung Fu, Pentjac Silat and the fighting arts of the Philippines, Hawaiian Islands and Western methods of combat. Quite a variety of martial arts have been mentioned as a few of the systems practiced in the world. I have become acquainted with many of the masters and leaders and also include the Russian methods in which fighting was perceived.

There is really no one art better than another. It all depends on how a practitioner of any style devotes his time and energy to his art. As I dwell through my endeavors on a daily basis of staying mentally and physically productive, I would like to clarify my vision in seeing a picture of the whole wide world. I honor and respect people for their efforts in keeping the martial arts going, no matter what system they are practicing.

I thank God most sincerely that I was never a fighting arts great, but only a man who enjoys life, family and friends. And one who admires the great martial arts masters at work.

–The Author

16317677R00112

Made in the USA
San Bernardino, CA
27 October 2014